GANDHI,
Soldier of Nonviolence

GANDHI, Soldier of Nonviolence

An introduction

Calvin Kytle

SEVEN LOCKS PRESS

Cabin John, Md. / Washington, D.C.

ACKNOWLEDGMENT

Our special thanks to the Information Service, Indian Consulate, New York City, and to the Press Information Bureau, Embassy of India, Washington, D.C., for their gracious assistance and cooperation.

Photo Credits: Bettmann Archive, 52, 77, 106. Brown Brothers, 45, 49, 57, 85, 93, 117. Culver Pictures, Inc., 11, 12, 33, 38, 95, 121, 126, 130, 133. Embassy of India, 2, 20, 78, 98, 105, 110, 151, 153, 163, 167, 168, 176, 183, 195. Indian Consulate, 25, 67, 71, 143, 180, 189. New York Public Library, 14, 16, 62, 158, 167, 184. Underwood & Underwood, 82. Wide World Photos, 5, 6, 8, 10, 44, 124, 137, 146–47, 175, 178, 186.

Library of Congress Cataloging in Publication Data
Kytle, Calvin.
  Gandhi, soldier of nonviolence.

  Bibliography: p.
  Includes index.
  1. Gandhi, Mahatma, 1869–1948. 2. Nonviolence. 3. Statesmen — India — Biography. I. Title.
DS481.G3K9   1983   954.03′5′0924   82-10633
ISBN 0-932020-18-6
ISBN 0-932020-19-4 (pbk.)

Book design by Chuck Myers
Manufactured in the United States of America

SEVEN LOCKS PRESS, INC.
Publishers
P.O. Box 72, Cabin John, Maryland 20181

Distributed to the trade by Everest House, Inc., Publishers, 33 West 60th Street, New York 10023

Note: A slightly different version of this book was published by Grosset & Dunlap in 1969 under the title *Gandhi, Soldier of Nonviolence: His Effect on India and the World Today.* For this Seven Locks edition the author has written a new preface and made a few textual revisions, notably in Chapter One.

To the memory of Martin Luther King, Jr.

Author's Preface

At last count nearly 450 books had been published about Gandhi, most of them biographies. Besides their subject, what the authors would seem to have most in common is their boldness. The Mahatma's chief political disciple and India's first prime minister, Jawaharlal Nehru, once said plainly that the only person qualified to write about Gandhi would have to be "as big as Gandhi." He obviously meant Gandhi himself.

Nehru's opinion to one side, the fact is that Gandhi's life was so complex, so full, and so rich in meaning that only a person of prodigious talent and endless perseverance could possibly hope to capture the man whole. Fortunately, there is something in Gandhi for everybody. Whatever the professional persuasion or point of view — be it that of political scientist, theologian, fund raiser, lawyer, sociologist, psychiatrist, nutritionist, propagandist, or mystic — no writer taking up the subject need ever be at a loss for material. Because Gandhi is a man of infinite fascination and because, as time goes on, the facts of his life will need to be regularly separated from enveloping myths, we can confidently expect even more books about him.

Still, no writer venturing a new book on Gandhi and wanting to invest his or her work with the honesty and candor of its subject can escape the question implicit in the ever-lengthening list in *Books in Print*: "Why still another book about this already copiously documented life?" So, a word about *Gandhi, Soldier of Nonviolence*:

In slightly different form, this book first appeared in 1969, on the occasion of the one-hundredth anniversary of Gandhi's birth. I was commissioned by Grosset & Dunlap to do the book as one in a new series to be called "Crosscurrents of the Twentieth Century." The series was aimed at what at the time was thought to be a promising new mar-

ket, the so-called young adult market, meaning eleventh
and twelfth graders.

According to the original concept, mine was to be pri-
marily a book about Gandhi's influence on the civil-rights
movement. This was a matter with which I had more than
passing familiarity; for the year preceding I had been immersed in conflict resolution, both in theory and practice,
as deputy director of the U.S. Community Relations Service, the federal conciliation agency set up by the 1964 Civil
Rights Act. Before I had gone through a first draft,
however, Grosset faced one of its periodic and traumatic
changes in ownership, a new editor for the series was
brought in, and I was told that the publisher now wanted
a straightforward biography. At this point, I had to ask
myself: "What possible value could there be in a book about
Gandhi, written by a man who had never met him, never
been to India, and whose entire knowledge of *Satyagraha*
and the Free India movement derived from newspapers and
newsreels?"

The question drove me deeper into the Library of Congress. There I discovered two things:

One, most of the books about Gandhi written for American readers concentrated on his life after his return to India from South Africa in 1914. Relatively little attention
was given to his twenty years in Africa which, on examination, struck me as being a real-life rehearsal for what
was to come in India. The more I read, the greater my
conviction: One could begin to understand how Gandhi
came to hold the views he did — indeed, how and why he
was able to transform himself into India's Great Soul —
only if one first understood what happened to Gandhi, and
what he caused to happen, during his time in Africa.

Two, the story of these formative years was available
in abundant detail from Gandhi himself, in his autobiography covering the period from his birth to 1921.

It would, I decided, be eminently worth doing merely
to distill this story of his youth and growth in a way that
young Americans could relate to.

This book, then, represents my conscientious effort to provide a concise, unpretentious primer, faithful both to the record and to Gandhi's spirit, with an emphasis on those things that I thought would be most appealing to young Americans coming of age in the seventies — Gandhi's growth in self-awareness, the development of his social policies, and the testing of his nonviolent political strategies. That the first edition seems to have been received as such by as many old adults as young ones has been gratifying. I can only hope that this new version will serve to introduce the man to more Americans, of whatever age, and that they might then be moved to study him in fuller dimension. For this purpose, readers might find useful the bibliography on page 191.

The bibliography names most of the works that, along with contemporary periodicals, I used to augment Gandhi's personal account. To enhance readability, I have by and large dispensed with individual citations for the direct quotations from Gandhi himself. Unless otherwise stated, they are all drawn from one of three volumes: his autobiography, *The Story of My Experiments With Truth,* published in the United States by Beacon Press in 1957; *All Men Are Brothers,* an excellent, almost epigrammatic treatment of his speeches and writings, published by UNESCO in 1958; and *The Essential Gandhi,* a usefully annotated anthology edited by Louis Fischer and published by Random House in 1962.

My wife Elizabeth was consistently helpful in my attempt to keep the book as free of non-essentials as Gandhi kept his life. Prahful Shah reviewed the manuscript from the invaluable viewpoint of a man who not only knew India but was close to members of the Gandhi family. Kanu Gandhi, the Mahatma's grandson, has read the finished book and commends it for accuracy. My thanks to them all.

Calvin Kytle
Washington, D.C.
July 1982

"Yours is the heaven that lies in the common dust, and you are there for me, and you are there for all."

—TAGORE

"The light that shone in this country was no ordinary light; the light that has illumined this country for many years will illumine this country for many more years still, and a thousand years later that light will still be seen in this country, and the world will see it, and it will give solace to innumerable hearts, for that light represented something more than the immediate present; it represented the living truth."

—JAWAHARLAL NEHRU

Contents

GANDHI,
Soldier of Nonviolence

Mahatma Gandhi, affectionately called "Bapu" (father) by his followers.

ONE

The Mahatma's Beckoning Truth

Mohandas Gandhi was in his lifetime, and remains in death, a puzzle to the world.

The one thing that can be said with certainty is that he belongs to that small number of great men who cannot be pigeonholed, catalogued, summed up, pinned down, or in any way easily explained.

He was so thin, so bony, that he looked as if he might snap in two when the next wind blew. In reality, his body was as supple as his character. He bent. He never broke.

Until Gandhi came along, civil disobedience had been the proud act of an individual conscience. He made it an instrument of mass protest, powerful enough to rock an empire.

He not only mixed politics with religion; he mixed religions. "I do not share the belief that there can or will be on earth one religion," he said. "I am striving to find a common factor and to induce mutual tolerance."

But to those who saw in his teachings the emergence of a new faith, he said, "There is no such thing as Gandhism." And to those who would make him a saint, he said, "I am not a saint who has strayed into politics. I am a politician who is trying to become a saint."

During one of the most violent periods in the most violent century in history, he insisted that "nonviolence is the law of

3

our species." To those who scoffed, he said: "You say there can be no nonviolent rebellion and there has been none known to history. Well, it is my ambition to provide an instance." And he did.

He was a natural fighter but a born peacemaker, a socialist whose aim was to make every man a capitalist, a nationalist who refused "to hurt England to serve India." He was a cheerful man who based a movement on humanity's capacity for suffering. He was a man who campaigned for freedom by asking his enemies to put him in jail. Above all, he was a man who tried to practice what he preached — which is perhaps why, to men long accustomed to saying one thing and doing another, he was a hopeless bundle of contradictions.

Throughout Gandhi's lifetime, people found it easier to like him than to understand him. Today, years after his death, historians find it easier to acknowledge his achievements than to agree on their assessment of them.

Their quarrel is not over the importance of his leadership in the long fight for Indian independence. It is over the validity and impact of his nonviolent method. Was he, as some claim, the bearer of *the* truth that will finally set men free? Or was he, as others maintain, a freak, an impostor, the purveyor of an outrageously false and dangerous idea? Was his victory of only momentary significance, possible of achievement only among Indians and only against the British? Or was it, as Count Leo Tolstoy said in 1910, "the most important of all the work now being done in the world wherein not only the nations of the Christian but of all the world will inevitably take part"?

Without question, what Gandhi succeeded in doing in India had a decidedly moderating influence on the European colonial powers after World War II. The Indian experience established a pattern by which all the nationalist movements in Asia and Africa could be peaceably accommodated. Between 1956 and 1965 more than fourteen African nations achieved their independence. In all but two — Algeria and Rhodesia — freedom came without violence.

"It may be through American Negroes that the unadulterated message of nonviolence will be delivered to the world," Gandhi once told an American visitor, and for a while it looked as if he might be right. For ten years, led by Dr. Martin Luther King, Jr., American blacks submitted passively to billy clubs, police dogs, electric cattle prods, mounted vigilantes, bombings, and imprisonment in a relentless round of sit-ins, kneel-ins, freedom rides, and marches. It was almost entirely because of their efforts that the Civil Rights Acts of 1964 and 1965 were passed, bringing to an end legalized racial segregation in the United States.

Dr. King took pains to acknowledge his indebtedness to Gandhi. As a result, during the sixties Gandhi entered the honored company of American freedom-fighters. Between *Swaraj* in India and "Freedom Now" in America, between Soul Force *(Satyagraha)* and Soul Power, between Gandhi's March to the Sea and Dr. King's March to Montgomery, events have drawn a secure connection. Black Americans have read of how, in 1893, a white conductor threw Gandhi off a railway coach, forcing him

Count Leo Tolstoy,
Russian author famous for "War and Peace," renounced his wealth and tried to live a life of simplicity based on the brotherhood of man.

to make the decision that led to his organizing the Indian revolution. They consider it no mere coincidence that their own revolution began in 1955 when Rosa Parks, a middle-aged Negro seamstress, refused to give up her bus seat to a white man.

But as an organizing principle of black protest, nonviolence was reduced to apparent irrelevance in August 1965 when accumulated rage and frustration exploded in the Watts area of Los Angeles, leaving thirty-four persons dead, a thousand-odd injured, and six hundred buildings destroyed. The riot touched off a series of summer disorders, each accompanied by extensive burning and looting, in the black ghettos of virtually every big northern city in America. Less than three years later Martin Luther King, Jr., was dead of an assassin's bullet.

Since then the record has hardly been one to support the Tolstoy prophecy. Personal and mob violence has increased, as if in direct ratio to the increase in the earth's population. In-

Dr. Martin Luther King, Jr., leads marchers near Montgomery, Alabama. On his left is his wife Coretta, and behind him singer Harry Belafonte. The nonviolent U.S. civil rights movement under Dr. King's leadership owed its inspiration, and much of its strategy, to Gandhi.

cidents of international terrorism have become so common they can no longer be considered merely the bizarre acts of a deranged few. Unrelieved conflict between Arabs and Jews in the Middle East and between Catholics and Protestants in Northern Ireland do not testify to a growth in brotherly love. And while demonstrations of a sort that Gandhi would have called aggressive non-violence may have helped change U.S. policy in Vietnam, civil disobedience now seems plainly out of fashion.

In the light of recent history, some writers tend to sum up Gandhi by examining his achievements in terms of his own stated goals and by reducing these goals to two. One of his goals, they point out, was to free India of English rule; the other was "to convert every Indian, every Englishman, and finally the world" to brotherhood and nonviolence. The first goal he achieved spectacularly. But that he failed in his second mission, they say, is plainly evidenced by the world's continuing reliance on warfare.

And yet, and yet. Human progress does not move in a constant ascent. People neither learn nor change without forgetting and falling back. Just as corruption in time repels, so too does virtue pall. Good and powerful ideas do not die. They only wait for another cause and a fresh surge of human energy. And so it may be that the ideas Gandhi spent his life exemplifying may be on the verge, once again, of animating a popular movement and informing a significant public debate. A motion picture of incomparable spectacle — produced by an Englishman, financed in part by the Indian government, and distributed internationally by an American film company — promises to make his teachings credible to a brand-new generation and to fix him permanently in the mass imagination as a planetary folk hero. And with the revival of fears of a nuclear holocaust and demands for a nuclear freeze, his theories of conflict resolution are sure to be seen more and more not only as a reasonable option in the search for disarmament but as offering in the long run the only practical alternative to war.

And so it is — still another paradox — that Gandhi is now coming to be remembered more for his "failure" than for his presumed victory. What's more, among those who remember him best are the fretful men in high places who during his lifetime rejected his philosophy even as they were obliged to accept its political effects. They have forgotten that Winston Churchill once called him "a seditious fakir." They have come to call him Mahatma — Great Soul — as if it were his given name, in involuntary agreement with the Hindus who gave him the title. Increasingly, in a world dominated by war and threats of war, the memory of Gandhi nags uncomfortably at the minds of statesmen and generals — a strange, wasted figure in a loincloth, dark brown eyes gleaming behind enormous glasses, too kind to say, "I told you so," but remonstrating nonetheless, standing somewhere in the distance like a beckoning truth, waiting for the world to catch up.

Winston Churchill once called Gandhi a "seditious fakir."

TWO

India Under British Rule

To appreciate the scale of Gandhi's achievement—to understand why he was victorious even in defeat—it helps to bear this in mind:

Everything about the India of his day—its geography, its history, its religious culture, its politics—made it a country easier to free than to unite.

Twenty times the size of Great Britain and half the size of the United States, India sprawls from the protecting Himalayas in the north to the Indian Ocean in the south. At one extreme is eternal snow, at the other scorching heat. In some areas the monsoons bring yearly floods. In others, there is perpetual drought.

In Gandhi's day, the country was divided politically between eleven British provinces—some as large as a single European nation—and five hundred and sixty-two small princely states, which existed in relative independence through the grace of the Crown. Less than a fourth of the total population lived in the principalities. But for the ninety out of every hundred who lived in the rural villages, it made little difference whether they were subjects of the Empire or of a native rajah. In the seven hundred thousand villages (on the average, each consisted of five hundred acres and between fifty to a hundred families), life went on

Monsoon: A striking aerial view of flooded villages near Delhi after heavy rains caused the Jamuna River to overflow its banks.

without change, as it had for half a century. Sugar cane was crushed in hand mills. The soil was tilled with wooden plows. The people lived in huts of mud and thatch that had neither windows nor chimneys. Their cattle lived with them. There were no paved roads and no running water. Sewage ran along narrow alleyways.

Yet, colonial India contained Calcutta, the second largest city in the British Empire. Here, as in the big cities of

Bombay, Madras, Cawnpore, and Ahmedabad, the rich and
the poor, the East and the West, the old, new, and all possible variations thereof, were evident in dazzling profusion.
On the bustling streets well-dressed Englishmen mingled
with Hindus wearing loincloths, the traditional *dhoti*. Hand-
some carriages shared the thoroughfares with sacred cows
and bullock carts, hawkers screamed their wares in front
of smart western-styled shops, and at night thousands of
half-naked men, with no place else to go, slept on the pave-
ments. Interspersed with the magnificent government buildings, the hospitals, the banks, and the factories were slums
of unimaginable filth, congestion, and crime.

No privileged class ever lived in more unconscionable
splendor than India's storied maharajahs. In contrast,
throughout most of her history, life for India's masses has
been dominated by the constant threat of famine. During

In colonial India, Calcutta was the second largest city in the British Empire.
This is how it looked when Gandhi was young.

No privileged class ever lived in greater splendor than India's maharajahs. This mighty prince of yesterday held court in his palace near Delhi.

Gandhi's lifetime, the population grew from two hundred million to four hundred million, thanks largely to improved medical care and the absence of birth control. Still, an average of six million persons died every year from preventable diseases; until World War II, malaria alone killed a million a year. As late as 1941, sixty-five per cent of the people died before they were thirty.

India's population is fragmented, having three major ethnic groups—Mongoloid, Aryan, and Dravidian—and hundreds of lesser ethnic divisions. The problem of communications has always been formidable. To this day, India's people speak fourteen major languages and at least two hundred and fifty regional dialects.

There are seven major religious groups: Hindus, Moslems, Christians, Jains, Parsis, Sikhs, and Buddhists. Hindus comprise sixty-five per cent of the population, Moslems twenty-five per cent. The Hindu caste system serves to divide the population even more. Introduced three thousand years ago, the system became progressively complicated until it split into more than three thousand separate groups. In some intricate fashion these sub-castes relate to four main occupational categories, with the Brahmans at the top and the untouchables (about fifty million) at the bottom. When rigidly enforced, the system will not permit the member of one caste to marry, or even associate with, a member of another.

One must be careful in generalizing about Hinduism. It has no precise dogma and its teachings are broad enough to accommodate the most sophisticated disciple of God as well as the most primitive idol worshipper. According to orthodox Hinduism, the human soul goes through an infinitely long series of wanderings and earthly reincarnations, moving from body to body. Death, therefore, is seen only as an incident in a foreordained cycle of rebirths. Until Gandhi, this religiously grounded attitude of resignation toward death had defeated every native effort to improve living conditions in the here-and-now.

India's civilization goes back to at least 4000 B.C., making

13

MERCHANT

WARRIOR

PRIEST

ARTISAN

The Indian caste system is complicated and rigid. The four basic Hindu castes are the Brahmans (priests), the Kshatriyas (warriors), the Vaisyas (merchants), and the Sudras (artisans). The pariah people of India—the untouchables—are so low on the social scale that they do not even hold caste rank.

UNTOUCHABLE

it one of the oldest on record. But modern India dates only from the sixteenth century, when the Portuguese, followed closely by the Dutch, the French, and finally the British, began to organize commerce in the Far East. After that, the European influence spread quickly, reaching its climax in the middle of the eighteenth century when the British East India Company secured a virtual monopoly. By 1857, the entire Indian subcontinent was under British imperial control, either directly or by permissive treaty with the native princes.

Britain brought many reforms to India. It gave the country a kind of political unity for the first time, and, by requiring that English be the common language in the public schools, began to cultivate a corps of native leaders who could communicate with one another. It introduced an extremely efficient governmental system, dividing the country into twenty-five administrative districts, each presided over by a member of the Indian Civil Service, the *corps d'élite*. Rarely in history have so few ruled so effectively over so many. During the late nineteenth century less than a thousand Englishmen were employed in the government of 268 million Indians.

Under Britain, slave trading was forbidden; famine-control measures and semi-representative government were introduced; widow-burning (*sati*), ritual strangling (*thaqi*), infanticide, and other primitive rites were abolished; a public works department was set up; great roads, telegraph lines, railroads, and a postal service were built. The British also should be credited with introducing the world's first Equal Employment law. The 1833 act renewing the charter of the East India Company provided that "no Native of the said (Indian) territories nor any natural-born subject of his Majesty resident therein, shall, by reason only of his religion, place of birth, descent, colour, or any one of them be disabled from holding Place, Office, or Employment."

In fact, in the mid-1800s Britain seemed sincerely interested first in democratizing India, then in freeing her for self-government. One governor-general kept as his motto,

15

The Sepoy Rebellion—also known as the Indian Mutiny—broke out in 1857. Above, the rebels in a night attack on enemy baggage wagons; below, the mutineers shoot down a British officer.

16

"British Greatness upon Indian Happiness." Another went on record saying, "It will be England's greatest boast that she has used her sovereignty towards enlightening her subjects so as to enable the native communities to walk alone in the paths of justice."

But in 1857, Indian troops in the north revolted against their British officers and for more than a year there ensued what has since been known as the Indian Mutiny—a wildly disorganized episode of heroism, massacre, and brutality. When it was over, the British government promptly took over control from the East India Company and began a gradual reversal of the liberal movement, which but a few years before had offered so much promise. Most significant of all, the British ceased annexing the princely states on evidence of gross misrule, as had been their practice, and adopted a "hands-off" policy with respect to the ruling rajahs. For years thereafter, Britain pursued an ambiguous policy. Through its press, its missionaries, and its schools, the government assiduously promoted democracy, industrialism, and the humane values of Christianity. Meanwhile, through its alliances with the native princes, it legitimatized one of the most autocratic political systems in modern history.

Thus, at the time of Gandhi's birth, a kind of creative chemistry was at work in India, bringing together, sometimes explosively, the contradictory elements within two distinct cultures. The result was as unique as the mixture. There was no word for it. To express it truly, a symbol was needed. It was Gandhi's destiny to become that symbol.

THREE

The Young Mohandas

Mohandas Karamchand Gandhi was born on October 2, 1869, in Porbandar, a picturesque port town of about 70,000 people on the Kathiawar peninsula north of Bombay. Like some three hundred other small city-states in the Gujarat region, the town was ruled by a native prince whom the British usually left alone as long as he did what he was told.

The Gandhis belonged to the *Modh Bania* subdivision of the *Vaisya* caste. On the old Hindu social scale, the *Vaisyas,* all of whom are supposed to be tradesmen or farmers, ranked third and the *Bania,* which had a connotation of money-lender, slightly lower. The first Gandhis had been grocers; in fact, Gandhi means "grocer" in Hindi. But by the time of Mohan's birth, there were almost as many members of the family in official government positions as there were in trade. Gandhi's father, as his father had been before him, was *diwan,* or chief minister, for the Porbandar prince.

The youngest of six children, Mohan spent his early years in a three-story house that had been in the family since 1777. As an infant he could not always tell his brothers and sisters from his numerous cousins, for, following the Hindu custom, his father shared the house with five brothers, their children, and their children's children. The immediate family lived in two rooms—one of them twenty by thirty feet, the other thirteen by twelve. Patience and the ability to give and take, were the stuff of survival in such crowded quarters. Mohan learned both, plus a special knack for tuning out what he did not want to hear.

In later years Gandhi freely credited his mother with his religious bent. It apparently never occurred to him that he may have owed his father for something equally important—his instinct for practical politics and diplomacy. While officially the servant of the ruling prince, Karamchand Gandhi was really a negotiator—a sort of broker in grievances—among the native chiefs, British political agents, and the long-suffering subjects. Under the circumstances, it was remarkable that he held the job for twenty-eight years before falling victim to one of the recurrent state intrigues. When in 1876 his relations with the prince finally reached the breaking point, he managed to resign in such a way that he neither offended the court nor jeopardized his brother's chances to succeed him. He then moved the family to Rajkot, another city-state 120 miles east, where the ruling prince was happy to appoint him *diwan*.

Though poorly educated (he could read Gujarati at about the fifth-grade level), Gandhi's father had a common-sense approach to problems that made his judgment highly valued in official circles. He had a name for absolute loyalty. Once in his presence an assistant political agent for the British spoke insultingly of the Rajkot prince. While other members of the court sat in silence, Karamchand rose and reprimanded the agent. He was immediately arrested. Even under threat of long detention, he refused to apologize, thereby giving young Mohan his first lesson in passive resistance. Whether out of grudging admiration for Karamchand or out of his own fear of making too much of a scene, the exasperated agent released him after a few hours.

Karamchand—or Kaba as he was known to the children—had been widowed three times and was nearly fifty years old when Mohan was born. Putlibai, his fourth wife, was twenty years younger and an astonishingly active embodi-

19

Mohandas Gandhi as a child.

ment of the traditional Hindu virtues—love, humility, and self-sacrifice. She was a small, fragile-looking woman who, through a relentless force of will, was able to keep on a virtually uninterrupted round of fasts and vows and at the same time take care of her family, nurse the sick of the community, and listen sympathetically to the ladies of the palace. Young Gandhi spent virtually all his hours after school with her; accompanying her to the temple for prayer; squatting nearby, listening, as she comforted the widowed mother of the prince; helping her tend the sick, often throughout the night. He was as struck by her powers of endurance as he was awed by her spirit of willing self-denial, and she was undoubtedly his inspiration during some of the most troubled times of his adult life. "When he speaks of his mother," a friend observed in 1908, "his voice softens and the light of love is in his eyes."

In Porbandar, Mohan had made friends, spun tops, and played with balloons on the beach. He was something of a tease and a distinct trial to his older sister, who was charged with keeping an eye on him. He would distract her and then dart off and hide, write on the floor in chalk, and sometimes scatter the utensils of worship. More than once when her back was turned he removed the image of the ruling prince from a stool and seated himself in its place. Her shocked expression would send him off into wild fits of laughter. But he apparently dropped his playfulness when the family moved to Rajkot. In fact, to judge from his autobiography, he went through a period when he was almost morbidly shy. "My books and my lessons were my sole companions. To be at the school at the stroke of the hour and to run back home as soon as the school closed—that was my daily habit. I literally ran back, because I could not bear to talk to anybody." Until cricket and football were made compulsory, he played no games and, except for brisk, solitary walks, he took no exercise. His classmates, however, would occasionally call on him to arbitrate their quarrels. It was a role he seemed to enjoy.

Shortly after he turned thirteen, the Gandhi household was suddenly caught up in preparations for a coming event. Gandhi's father and uncle met almost daily, and though they talked mostly of money and expenses their mood was disconcertingly lighthearted. The women, meanwhile, were busy trying to outdo one another in clothes-making, ornament-making, and meal-planning. Plainly, something important was coming up. In time, although his parents acted as if he should understand without being told, Gandhi learned what it was. It was a wedding. To be precise, it was to be a triple wedding. For reasons of economy and convenience, the family had decided to marry him, his 15-year-old brother, and a 14-year-old cousin all at the same time.

He was so young that the prospect of marriage meant little more than good new clothes, drum-beating, processions, rich feasts, and a new playmate. About his bride-to-be he was told only that she was his own age, that her name was Kasturbai, and that she was the daughter of Gokaldass Mackanji, a Porbandar merchant. He may have met her once; if so, he could not remember. He and his brother were taken to Porbandar for the ceremonies. There he shed some of his shyness and, perhaps for the first time in his young life, was pleased to be the center of attention.

Once the festivities were done, however, the problems of being thirteen and also a husband almost undid him. Kasturbai was a lovely young girl but maddeningly independent.

21

It shamed and infuriated him that she showed no fear of the dark, whereas he could not bear to sleep in an unlighted room. She was illiterate and, as much to show his superiority as to educate her, he tried to teach her to read. But the only times he could be with her were at night, for Kathiawar then had its own strict and peculiar *purdah,* which effectively confined Kasturbai to the company of women during the day. Furthermore, though a charming pupil, she was a decidedly unwilling one. As a result, the nightly lessons almost invariably ended when, exasperated and aroused, he would announce that he would rather make love.

For advice on how to be a better husband, he turned to a series of popular pamphlets on such subjects as wedlock, thrift, and home-making. While none of their counsel was lost on him, they had their greatest effect in convincing him of his duty to be faithful to Kasturbai. At the same time, they filled him with an obsessive fear that Kasturbai might not be faithful to him. Driven by an unreasoning jealousy, he ordered her never to go anywhere without his permission. She ignored him. She went whenever and wherever she liked. The more he tried to restrict her, the more she defied him. They went for days without speaking. Finally, she won.

Otherwise, Gandhi's teens were marked by the same uncertainties, the same spirit of uneasy rebellions typical of adolescents anywhere. They differed only to the degree that his curiosity was greater than average and in that he might have had a somewhat compulsive tendency to moralize. He and a venturesome young relative experimented briefly with smoking, stealing cigarettes from the servants and sometimes stealing pennies to buy them with. Once when both were afflicted with a sudden fit of romanticism and self-pity, they decided to kill themselves, going so far as to swallow two or three seeds of a poisonous jungle plant. At fifteen, he stole a bit of gold out of his brother's armlet. Seized with remorse, he wrote out a confession, handed it to his father, and asked to be punished. To his surprise, Kaba did not react in anger but wept and offered his forgiveness. Mohan wept too and promptly drew a moral: "A clean confession, combined with a promise never to commit the sin again, when offered before one who has the right to receive it, is the purest type of repentance."

Underlying these youthful acts of testing and self-exploration was a serious and troubled questioning of religion. It was never his nature to accept on faith whatever he was told. Even as a small child he had been unsatisfied with the answers his mother gave him to questions like, "Why would I be contaminated if I were to have contact with an untouchable?" Though he went regularly to the *Haveli*—the Vaishnava temple—he instinctively resisted the dogmatic teachings of the priests there. He had been impressed too often with the "truths" of too many diverse branches of the Hindu faith to believe that any one of them had all the answers.

For a while, his search for a definition of God led him to question the very existence of God. He read *Manusmriti,* "The Laws of Manu," hoping to find in it something he could believe in, but was confused all the more. The book, a complex one to which religious scholars have given widely varying interpretations, seemed to contradict many of the basic tenets of Hinduism. It seemed to Mohan that Manu's laws even permitted meat-eating. When, distressed, he went to an older and highly intellectual cousin, he was told merely to stop asking questions: "When you grow older you will be able to solve these doubts yourself."

Young Mohan decided that his cousin was right, that perhaps everything would come clear to him when he grew up. So, relieved, he deferred the question, "Is there a God?" and instead put his faith in a proposition: that "morality is the basis of things and . . . truth the substance of all morality." Years later the proposition would become the premise for a revolutionary political strategy.

Gandhi's older brother, Karsandas, had a Moslem friend, a classmate named Sheik Mehtab, whom most of the family viewed as the Bad Boy of Rajkot. Sheik was big, muscular, a star high-jumper, and something of a show-off. Though his teachers often had reason to paddle him, and did, the beatings never fazed him. He told jokes on the British. He bragged of his visits to brothels. He drank wine unashamedly. Wine, he told his awed and admiring schoolmates, was good for the blood. To show how little he feared snakes, he would pick them up and hold them in his palms. And what to his allowance-short classmates was even more impressive, Sheik always had money in his pockets. Young Gandhi, who saw himself as shy, scared, and a weakling, was dazzled by him. He could think of nothing better than to be like him.

To be like him, however, would require that Mohan eat meat. In fact, Sheik had developed a long, elaborate rationale that virtually equated meat-eating with patriotism. "Look," he would say to Mohan, "we are weak people because we do not eat meat. The English can rule over us because they do."

He would then recite a bit of popular doggerel:

"Behold the mighty Englishman
He rules the Indian small,
Because being a meat-eater
He is five cubits tall."

"You know how hardy I am," Sheik went on. "It's because I eat meat. Meat-eaters do not have boils or tumors. Our teachers who eat meat are no fools."

Our *teachers?* Mohan was shocked. Of course, said Sheik, and he would tick off the names. "They know its virtues," Sheik continued. "You should do likewise. Try it and see."

After several such conversations, Mohan felt himself being carried away. Confused, he turned to Karsandas, expecting now to hear the other side. But Karsandas only smiled and flexed his muscles. He had been eating meat secretly for months, he said. Convinced, Mohan agreed to join them.

Kasturbai, Putlibai, and his eldest brother, Laxmidas, all tried to talk him out of his new friendship. He countered with an argument that he came halfway to believe: "He cannot lead me astray, as my association with him is meant to reform him."

24

With his brother Laxmidas; the future Mahatma (right) is seventeen here.

Where, in fact, Sheik led him was to a hidden spot by the river. There Gandhi saw meat for the first time in his life. At Sheik's coaxing, he proceeded to eat it, cramming his mouth with baker's bread before every swallow. It was goat's meat and as tough as leather. He began to retch, in part from the taste but mostly out of nervousness. Too sick to eat more than a few bites, he begged off.

That night, every time he dropped off to sleep, he dreamed that a live goat was bleating inside him. The nightmares, and the resulting remorse, were almost enough to make him quit the whole experiment. But having persuaded himself that meat-eating was his duty (for how else would the Brit-

25

ish be overcome?), he could not easily back out simply because his first attempt had made him ill. Furthermore, his friend was not of a disposition to give in. The next thing Mohan knew, Sheik was taking him to a private room in a public dining hall. Sheik had made arrangements in advance with the chief cook and this time, instead of goat's meat and plain bread, Gandhi found a variety of expertly prepared meat delicacies. He liked them; the goat meat was so disguised with savory sauces that it was easy for him to forget the goat.

These clandestine meat dinners continued for the course of a year. There were, all told, no more than a half dozen of them because the dining hall was not always available and because the expense proved taxing even to Sheik's means, as liberal as they were. But for the worry they caused him, Mohan might as well have had meat three times a day. After such a meal he had no appetite for dinner at home. "Come, eat your dinner," his mother would say as he entered the front door. He would try to look nauseated—which wasn't hard to do—and say, "There is something wrong with my digestion." Whereupon Putlibai would insist on nursing him, which compounded his anxiety all the more. Finally, the sneaking and the lying became too much. "So, I said to myself, though it is essential to take up food reform in this country, deceiving your father and mother is worse than not eating meat . . . When they are no more and I have found my freedom, I will eat meat openly, but until that moment arrives, I will abstain."

Shortly thereafter, Gandhi's father, Karamchand, came down with a fistula that would not heal. Ointments, plasters, and all known local nostrums failed. When an English surgeon recommended an operation, Karamchand went to Bombay expecting to have it performed. The family physician, however, objected because of Karamchand's advanced age. So Karamchand came back to Rajkot, took to his bed, and waited for death.

Mohan, Putlibai, and an old servant of the house spelled one another as nurse. For two years Gandhi's evening routine hardly varied. Home from school, he would go to his father's room, dress the wound, and mix whatever drugs were called for. Night after night, without neglect, he would massage his father's legs, then sit with him, sometimes reading aloud, until his father dozed off.

It was not easy for him. He loved his father, but as time went on he came to feel more and more resentful at having to spend all his evenings in a sickroom. Moreover, Kasturbai was pregnant and he was impatient to be with her. He was shocked by his own feelings. "Every night whilst my hands were busy massaging my father's legs, my mind was hovering about the bedroom."

When it became clear that Kaba was failing, Gandhi's uncle, Tulsidas, came from Porbandar to be with him. One night at about 11 o'clock Gandhi was giving his father his nightly massage when Tulsidas offered to relieve him. Grateful, Gandhi went immediately to his bedroom. He was annoyed to find Kasturbai asleep. How could she sleep, he asked himself, when *he* was there? He undressed quickly, woke her up and pulled her toward him.

Less than ten minutes later, there was a knock on the door.

"Get up," a servant shouted. "Get up!"

Gandhi sprang out of bed.

"What is it? What's the matter?"

His father was dead.

Not long after, their first child was born. It lived for only three or four days.

Now, for 17-year-old Mohan, the time of mourning became a time of guilt and soul-searching. He felt absolutely miserable for having deserted his station during his father's critical hour. "If animal passion had not blinded me, I should have been spared the torture of separation from my father during his last moments," he wrote in his autobiography. "It is a blot that I have never been able to efface or forget." Similarly, he blamed himself—"this carnal lust" within himself—for the death of the baby: "I did not restrain myself, as I should have done."

He had learned that he could not always trust his emotions, and the lesson troubled him. His feelings for Kasturbai softened. He came to realize how much he had been demanding of her and with what dignity she had put up with it. "I learned the lesson of nonviolence from my wife," he told a friend years later. "Her determined resistance to my will on the one hand, and her quiet submissiveness to the suffering of my stupidity on the other, ultimately made me ashamed of myself and cured me of my stupidity in thinking that I was born to rule over her."

Still, he could not entirely rid himself of "dark doubts and suspicions," nor of "the shackles of lust." He was surprised at his impulses, his shifting moods. He was alternately quiet and restive, relaxed and driven. He was no longer as shy, submissive or introspective as he had thought himself to be. But neither was he clearly anything else. Try as he might, he could not bring himself into focus.

Karamchand left his family little property. His chief legacy was his reputation and first claim to the *diwanship* for a son who could qualify.

At eighteen, Gandhi suddenly realized that Laxmidas and Putlibai were regarding him as the son most likely to succeed. Unlike Karsandas, who had quit school after marrying, he had lost only a year and, fortunately, he had been able to make it up by skipping a grade. He had, moreover, passed his matriculation examination in 1887 and was enrolled at Samaldas College in nearby Bhavnagar. But, unknown to his family, for most of the first term he was in a state of near panic. The courses were taught in English, which he had difficulty following; the professors were more demanding than the high-school teachers he had been accustomed to; and the subject matter was over his head. Sick with fear of failing, he came home during the first vacation, wondering how to face the family and whether it would be even worth the effort to go back for a second term. No wonder, then, that he responded so readily to a suggestion that he quit Samaldas and study abroad—especially when the suggestion came from a man who was both a learned Brahman and an old, trusted friend of his father's.

Making the argument to Laxmidas and Putlibai, Mavji Dave was quite persuasive. If Mohan were to stay in India it would take him five or six years to get a B.A. degree, he said. That would be sufficient to qualify him, at most, for a clerical post. On the other hand, by going to England, he could become a barrister in about three years and at considerably less expense. "He could get the *diwanship* for the asking!"

Gandhi could not conceal his eagerness. He would be pleased to go to England, he said. The sooner the better. But it was not a decision to be made lightly. Laxmidas, who was a lawyer in the prince's employ, recognized the value of a British degree but was uncertain that the family could stand the expense of keeping him in England for three years. Putlibai's concern was different. She had heard that young men got lost in England. They took to meat, she had been told; they could not live there without liquor.

"How can I trust you in a distant land?" she wanted to know. "I am dazed and do not know what to do."

She explained her dilemma to a Jain monk who had been close to her husband. The monk listened reflectively. "I shall get the boy solemnly to take three vows," he said, while Mohan held his breath. "Then he can be allowed to go." Under oath, Mohan then pledged to abstain from women, wine, and meat. With that, his mother gave him her blessing.

Laxmidas managed to raise the money (Gandhi had feared he might have to sell Kasturbai's jewels) and for a while it looked as if everything was going his way. Kasturbai bore him another son, this one marvelously alive and healthy. The Rajkot high school, few of whose graduates had been privileged to study in England, gave him a good-bye party. It was such a joyous occasion that it did not seem to matter that when he rose to speak the few words of thanks he had so painstakingly prepared he was struck dumb with stage fright.

Arriving in Bombay, where he was to catch the steamer, he was told that the Indian Ocean was unusually rough during the summer months and was advised to wait until fall for a safer passage. Though he had to wait several months for the seas to calm, he was too excited, too tense with anticipation, to feel lonely. By now he had come to view the journey to England as if it had been predestined. Nothing could stop him.

Perhaps this is why, uncharacteristically, he was so undaunted when he received a summons to appear before a general meeting of his caste — a meeting called expressly to consider the propriety of what he was proposing to do.

Before all the elders of the community, he was reminded by the *Sheth* (the head man) that the Hindu religion forbade voyages abroad. Indeed, no *Modh Bania* had ever been to England. "We have heard that it is not possible to live there without compromise," the *Sheth* told him. "One is obliged to eat and drink with Europeans!"

Gandhi sat unmoved. "I cannot alter my resolve," he replied. "My father's friend and adviser sees no objection, and my mother and oldest brother have given me their permission."

"But will you disregard the orders of the caste?"

"I think the caste should not interfere."

The *Sheth* was as unaccustomed to such matter-of-fact defiance as Gandhi was surprised to hear himself talking so defiantly. The *Sheth* swore and ordered him treated henceforth as an outcaste. "Whoever helps him," he thundered, "or goes to see him off at the dock shall be punishable with a fine of one rupee, four annas!"

So the price of passage to England was to include excommunication! Strangely, Gandhi felt unaffected. The order's main effect was to prompt him to leave for England as soon as possible. He knew that the *Sheth* would try to bring pressure on Laxmidas; the longer he stayed in Bombay the greater the chance that his brother and mother could be persuaded to withdraw their permission. He did not hesitate, therefore, when he learned that a ship was scheduled to sail for England early in September. In a frenzy of activity, he bought a steamer ticket, a tie, a short British jacket (though he thought it immodest), and enough fruit and sweets to last the three weeks to Southampton. He sailed on September 4, 1888, a month before his nineteenth birthday. He would be gone three years.

FOUR

The London Years

In his autobiography, Gandhi plays down his London period, relegating it to "the years before I began to live." He persistently describes himself as shy, ridiculous, self-conscious, and clumsy. He refers to himself repeatedly as "a coward."

Unhappily, most of his biographers have behaved as if it would be irreverent to dispute him. One of them, commenting on Gandhi at twenty-one, calls him "mediocre, unimpressive, handicapped, floundering." Another represents him as "earnest but diffident . . . with a limited range of interests." The commonly perpetuated idea is that he did nothing in London, and nothing happened to him there, to foreshadow the twentieth-century Mahatma. Louis Fischer saw no hint of "the real Gandhi" emerging, and B. R. Nanda, a more recent and equally friendly biographer, wrote: "Not even the most partial observer could have detected in this young barrister-at-law any promise of distinction . . . He did not seem to be cut out for a brilliant career, least of all in law or in politics."

This is, at best, a half truth. There may have been few signs of future greatness in the student Gandhi. But to picture him as mediocre, aimless, and perpetually tongue-tied is to ignore a good part of the record. Above all, he was

The University of London (left), where Gandhi was a law student. On the right stands the famous Victoria and Albert Museum.

no coward, no matter how often he may have felt like one. Indeed, if one can resist the temptation to seek signs of the leader he was to become and merely look at him plainly as the green youth that he was, the story of Gandhi in London shapes up as something of a triumph. Consider:

He entered a strange new world the moment he crossed the gangplank. Except for the passenger with whom he shared a cabin, everybody in the second saloon was English. His knowledge of the language was scanty, restricted almost entirely to the written word. When, in an overture of friendship, somebody addressed him, he could only stand dumb in embarrassment and try to convey with gestures that he did not understand. In the dining room, he was confused by the place-settings and too timid to inquire which dishes were free of meat. Rather than help him, the English passengers teased him, telling him among other things that once the ship entered the Bay of Biscay he would have to eat meat or be prepared to die. After a few days, he became so painfully self-conscious that he took to eating in his cabin, confining his meals to the fruits and sweets that he had brought with him. By the time the boat docked in Southampton, he was half-starved.

When he went to register at the University of London he was told it would be a month before he could begin his studies there. Fortunately, an Anglo-Indian friend of his father's suggested he spend the time in an "apprenticeship," practicing his English in the company of somebody sympathetic and learning the customs of an English household from the inside. It was then arranged for him to room with an Englishman in a boarding house in Richmond, a London suburb. For Gandhi, it would have been an altogether happy circumstance—his English improved rapidly and his new friend seemed genuinely eager to answer questions—except for one thing: he never got enough to eat.

The landlady was at a loss to know what to prepare for him. He had oatmeal for breakfast, which was fairly filling. But his lunches and suppers consisted almost entirely of boiled spinach and bread with jam. He could not relish potatoes without salt or condiments, it never occurred to the landlady to serve milk except with cereal, and Gandhi did not think it good manners to ask for more than two or three slices of bread.

His dilemma was acute. There were several schools of vegetarianism. One permitted both fish and eggs; one forbade fish but permitted eggs. The strict faith to which Gandhi's mother subscribed allowed neither. To be faithful to his vow, therefore, he had to be sure that the food he ate contained neither meat nor eggs. In restaurants he could rarely tell from the menu and the necessity to ask a waiter always embarrassed him. What made his discomfiture even worse, he was not, at that time, a vegetarian by principle. When challenged, he could offer no ready defense.

His friend argued with him at virtually every meal. "What's the value of a vow made before an illiterate mother and in ignorance of conditions here?" he would say. "You confess to having eaten and relished meat. You took it where it was absolutely unnecessary, and will not where it is quite essential. What a pity!" When it became obvious that Gandhi was neither to be bullied nor exhorted into changing his diet, the friend began reading aloud from books on logic. He quit only when, driven close to tears, Gandhi said vehemently and with clear finality: "I am helpless. A vow is a vow."

He took to taking long walks—partly in search of a vegetarian restaurant, partly because he had convinced himself that exercise would not only help keep up his strength but help divert his mind. He walked so fast that to most observers he appeared to be trotting. He rarely covered less than ten miles a day.

On one such excursion he spied a vegetarian restaurant in Farringdon Street. He was so glad, so relieved, he could hardly contain himself. He had his first full meal in three months.

At that same restaurant he bought a copy of Salt's *Plea for Vegetarianism*. He read it with quickening pulse, finding the discourse as gratifying as the food. It gave him a rationale he could believe in. In fact, he was immediately persuaded that a meatless diet was essential to good health. More, the book introduced him to the London Vegetarian Society. He need not be so lonely, nor feel so peculiar, after all. He had found a cause.

His conversion to vegetarianism had one interesting, if short-lived, side effect. At a restaurant one evening with his Richmond friend, he had refused to eat the soup until the waiter satisfied him it contained no meat. "You are too clumsy for decent society," his friend exploded. Thereupon, to please his friend, Gandhi decided to prove that one could be a vegetarian and still be fit for society. He would become an English gentleman.

So he discarded his suits of Bombay cut and bought new ones fashioned in London. He got his brother to send him a double watch chain of gold. He paid a Bond Street tailor ten pounds for an evening suit and put out nineteen shillings for a chimney-pot hat. With great effort, he changed the part in his thick black hair to the style of highborn young Englishmen.

To go with the new image, he invested in elocution lessons, French lessons, and dancing lessons. He bought a violin, found a teacher, and began to practice with the passion of a late-blooming prodigy. Finally, he became a party-goer.

Spying him one afternoon in Piccadilly Circus, an Indian acquaintance noted: "He was wearing a high silk hat burnished bright, a Gladstonian collar, stiff and starched; a rather flashy tie displaying almost all the colors of the rainbow, under which there was a fine silk striped shirt. He wore . . . a morning coat, a double-breasted vest and dark-striped trousers to match and not only patent leather boots but spats. He carried leather gloves and a silver-mounted stick. He was, to use the contemporary slang, a nut, a masher, a blood—a student more interested in fashion than in his studies."

But after three months of playing "the blood," Gandhi was afflicted with a terrible fit of self-consciousness. Try as he might, he could not make his feet keep time to the piano. He found that he had absolutely no aptitude for the violin and even less for the kind of small talk required at social gatherings. Moreover, throughout his foray into "polite society," he kept a meticulous accounting of his expenses, recording every farthing as he spent it and striking the balance at the end of the day. The nightly arithmetic soon sobered him. He realized that he was squandering money as well as time.

Rebounding, he moved into a cheaper room, swore to take a bus only in case of emergency, bought a stove, and began cooking his own meals. Before long, he had cut his living expenses to two pounds a month.

The cooking was, of course, an important exercise in his new vegetarian faith. He asked his family to stop sending him sweets and spices and began enjoying spinach and other vegetables without seasoning. Carrot soup became one of his specialties. He convinced himself that "the real seat of taste is not in the tongue but in the mind." As was to become more and more a rule of life for him, he found that his gratification in observing a vow was more than ample compensation for the privation and monotony.

He made a point of attending every meeting of the London Vegetarian Society. He helped design its badge, was elected to its executive committee, and as his English improved became a frequent contributor to its house organ, *The Vegetarian*. Membership in the Society was about evenly divided between food faddists and persons of sincerely religious motivation. Despite the fact that at the time he was mainly interested for reasons of health and economics, Gandhi found that he had more in common with those members who took the ethical view. Curiously, it was through such associations that he came to have his first intellectual appreciation for Hinduism as well as for Christianity.

Two brothers, both Theosophists, had been reading an English translation of *The Bhagavad-Gita* (Celestial Song), a sacred text of the Hindus. They asked Gandhi if he would help them read it in the original Sanskrit. He agreed, al-

Mme. Helena Blavatsky, whom Gandhi met in London, was a famous theosophist and spiritualist.

though he was embarrassed to confess that he had never read it in any version. It was an act of crucial discovery. Thereafter, for most of his adult years, he read from *The Gita* daily, regarding it as his "truth-book" and drawing from its verses the strength "to smile in the midst of overwhelming sorrow."

Through these same brothers, Gandhi met Madame H. P. Blavatsky and Mrs. Annie Besant and was induced to read their books on theosophy. But rather than convert him to theosophy, the acquaintance only increased his desire to know more about orthodox Hinduism. Mrs. Blavatsky's "Key to Theosophy" disabused his mind of the notion that Hinduism was rife with superstition, an idea fostered by the Christian missionaries he had heard on the streets of Rajkot.

Meanwhile, he came to think better of Christianity through the influence of a soft-spoken Bible salesman whom he met in a vegetarian boarding house. The salesman assured him that neither meat-eating nor wine-drinking was decreed in the Scriptures and pressed on him copies of the Old and New Testaments. Mostly out of politeness, Gandhi plodded through the Old Testament. He got through Genesis, was put to sleep by Leviticus, and actively disliked Numbers. But his interest picked up when he came to the New Testament, and after reading the Sermon on the Mount he felt as if he were home again. For here, restated, was the same principle of a Gujarati verse he had learned as a child:

"For a bowl of water, give a goodly meal;
For a kindly greeting bow thou down with zeal.
. . . But the truly noble know all men as one,
And return with gladness good for evil done."

Jesus's message delighted him: "Whosoever shall smite thee on thy right cheek, turn to him the other also. And if any man take away thy coat, let him have thy cloak too." Clearly, he decided, renunciation was the highest form of religion.

He became almost excessively conscientious about his studies. He was acutely aware of the inadequacy of his high-school education and especially sensitive to his need to master English. He decided, therefore, to take a high-school equivalency course. While continuing to read for the bar, he put himself through an intensive five-month discipline of study, preparatory to taking the matriculation examination at London University. He had to learn Latin and improve his French, for both were compulsory. He also took accelerated courses in chemistry and physics. On his first try, he failed the examination: "I ploughed Latin." But rather than lose heart, he went back to his books with renewed determination. Six months later, he took the examination and passed.

To qualify for the bar, two examinations were required,

one in common law, the other in Roman law. In preparation, most students read summaries or outlines, many of them successfully qualifying after only three months of concentrated study. Not Gandhi. He read the Roman law in Latin and spent nine months of hard labor working his way, cover-to-cover, through Broom's *Common Law,* Snell's *Equity,* Tudor's *Leading Cases,* and Edward's *Real Property.* He passed the examinations, was called to the bar on June 10, 1891, and enrolled in the High Court on June 11. He probably knew more English law than any Englishman enrolled with him.

He had reason to be proud of himself. Instead, he was loaded with misgivings. He lacked the one thing that every lawyer was assumed to have—the ability to speak in public.

He had tried earnestly to lose his stage fright, but virtually every attempt had been a repetition of his thank-you remarks to his classmates in Rajkot. To speak extemporaneously, as law students were encouraged to do, was absolutely out of the question. Even when he carefully wrote out every word in advance, it usually became necessary for somebody else to read what he had written. He would rise, his knees would tremble, his vision would blur; and when he opened his mouth the words either came out in a quick, almost unintelligible burst, or they never came out at all.

He had seen his last night in London as an opportunity to repay his friends for all their attentions. He arranged with the manager of The Holborn, a fashionable restaurant, to provide a strictly vegetarian dinner of special delicacy. He also had prepared an affecting little speech of farewell. He would open with a mild joke: a member of Parliament on his maiden speech in the House of Commons repeated "I conceive" three times, whereupon somebody in the audience said, "The gentleman conceived three times but brought forth nothing." The joke never got told. Gandhi stood up and, almost on cue, his knees began to shake, his vision blurred, and his throat went dry. Finally, after an almost superhuman effort, he was able to say, "Thank you,

gentlemen, for having kindly responded to my invitation."
After which he sat down in a near faint.

How, he asked himself, could he possibly manage in a
court of law where the ability to think and talk on his
feet could be a matter of life and death?

He sailed for Bombay on June 12, one day after his admission
to the High Court. After so long an absence, he was
eager to get home to Kasturbai and the family. It would be
especially satisfying to see his mother again. She would be
able to tell, just from the directness of his manner, that he
had kept his word. She, at least, would be proud of him.

Eight days after his departure, *The Vegetarian* carried his
assessment of his stay in England: "During my nearly three
years here, I have left many things undone. Yet I carry one
great consolation with me, that I shall go back without
having taken meat or wine, and that I know from personal
experience that there are so many vegetarians."

But more had happened to him in England than he
realized.

FIVE

Return to Bombay

Laxmidas was waiting for him when the boat docked in Bombay. Hardly were the greetings over when he was told that his mother had been dead a year. Knowing how much he loved her, the family had not informed him earlier for fear the news would distract him from his studies.

Grieving, Gandhi arrived in Rajkot wondering what other shocks were waiting for him. His son Harilal was four and a stranger. He found Kasturbai more beautiful than he remembered her and, to his dismay, he discovered that he was still as vulnerable as ever to fits of jealousy. Before other members of the family, he felt as if he were on exhibition.

The *Modh Bania,* he soon learned, was still unreconciled to his trip abroad. One section of the caste agreed to readmit him on the condition that he journey to Narvik and wash off his transgression with a dip in the holy waters of the Godavari. This he did, at the urgent suggestion of Laxmidas. Another section, however, refused to be appeased. Their laws of excommunication forbade his in-laws to entertain him; he could not so much as drink water in their homes.

But the hardest thing he had to cope with was the knowledge that Laxmidas, having strained the family's resources to give him a foreign education, was now expecting him to produce. The truth was, Gandhi was not yet qualified to produce. He had had no training in Indian law and a London degree alone meant absolutely nothing in the courts of Rajkot. Under the circumstances, it would have been foolish of him to start practice there. Not only did the locally trained *vakils* know Hindu and Moslem law like the backs of their hands; their fees were ten times lower than those that Gandhi, as a higher-ranked barrister, would have to charge.

He had no option but to go to Bombay. There he would have a chance to study Indian law, become familiar with the High Court, and, he hoped, pick up some income-yielding briefs. He stayed there only five months. The experience was a disaster.

His first case was a long time coming, perhaps because he considered it unprofessional to pay commissions to the touts on whom Indian lawyers routinely depended for business. When he did get a case, it turned out to be exactly as he feared. He was hired to defend a poor woman in the Small Causes Court; his fee was ten dollars. When he rose to cross-examine the plaintiff's witness, his heart sank, his head reeled, and he could think of no question to ask. The courtroom burst into laughter. As soon as he could pull himself together, he returned the fee and referred the woman to another lawyer. He felt disgraced.

He sought a part-time job as a high-school teacher. He was turned down because he had not graduated from an Indian University. Despairing, he learned that he could make a modest living writing legal petitions. It was the kind of work that required no appearances in court. But if this was what he was to be—a barrister's scribe—there was no point in his staying in Bombay, so he returned to Rajkot. There, thanks mostly to clients sent by his brother, he began to earn about a hundred dollars a month. A few months later—on October 28, 1882—his second son, Manilal, was born.

While in London, Gandhi had met the British Political Agent serving Kathiawar, and in a few subsequent social gatherings the two had become friends. This fact suddenly became very important. It seems that when secretary to the late Prince of Porbandar, Laxmidas had given some wrong

Law student. Soon he would grow a mustache to make himself look more mature.

advice, which his rivals had reported to the British agent as evidence of incompetence. As a consequence, Laxmidas stood to lose the *diwanship* for which he was in line.

Under pressure from Laxmidas, Gandhi called on the agent to plead his brother's case. The agent was cool, clearly suspicious that Gandhi was trying to exploit their brief acquaintance in London. When he learned the purpose of the visit, he became crisp and impatient.

"Your brother is an intriguer," he said angrily. "If he has anything to say in his defense, let him apply through proper channels."

Gandhi tried to explain. The agent rose and said tersely, as if giving an order: "You must go now." When, instead of leaving, Gandhi asked once again to be heard, the agent rang for a servant. The next thing Gandhi knew, he was being pushed out of the room.

It was Gandhi's first face-to-face encounter with a British

Bombay near the turn of the century, the city to which Gandhi went to study Indian law after his return from England.

official. Furious, he wrote the agent a note at once: "You have insulted me. If you make no amends, I shall have to proceed against you." Back by messenger came the agent's reply: "You are at liberty to proceed as you wish."

But there was no way, really, to proceed. Asked what he thought Gandhi should do, the leading lawyer in Bombay advised that he "tear up the note and pocket the insult." Gandhi was "still fresh from England and hot-blooded," he said. "He will gain nothing by proceeding against the *sahib*, and on the contrary he will very likely ruin himself."

Gandhi swallowed his pride, but the incident was enough to change the course of his life. He could not stand to play the willing toady. If this was to be the price of success in British-ruled India, then he would prefer to be an honest failure. Suddenly he was sick of Kathiawar—the petty intrigues, the open bribery, the ridiculous pomp and circumstance of the palace court, the subservience of his fellow Indians no less than the arrogance of the British. Once again, as he had five years before when he felt himself being overwhelmed, he wanted desperately to get away.

Escape came in 1893 with an offer from a firm of Porbandar Moslems. They had a substantial suit pending in South Africa. How would he like to represent them? He could expect to be gone a year. They would pay him 105 pounds and all expenses.

SIX

"The True Function of a Lawyer"

The civil suit that took Gandhi to South Africa was to be tried in Pretoria, in the Transvaal. Before taking up his assignment there, he spent a week or so in the port city of Durban, in Natal, 328 miles to the southeast. It was here that his client, a prosperous mercantile firm, Dada Abdulla & Co., had its headquarters.

The firm's president, Abdulla Sheth, was altogether kind but disturbingly vague about the job Gandhi had been hired to do. Abdulla told him only that the pending suit involved a claim of 40,000 pounds and that the company being sued was headed by a cousin of his, Tyeb Sheth. But was Gandhi to serve as counsel or as a clerk? Abdulla didn't know. He merely smiled and told Gandhi he was sure that his knowledge of English would prove to be helpful to the attorneys in Pretoria.

Abdulla's employees were a bit more informative, although what they told Gandhi hardly contributed to his peace of mind. The dispute was fundamentally a confusion of records, they said. The most telling aspects of the case could be understood only by a bookkeeper. Worried, Gandhi bought a textbook in accounting and began to study furiously. He mastered it in two days.

It was during these weeks in Durban that Gandhi had

47

his first exposure to legalized discrimination. To be sure, he had seen Europeans behave discourteously to Negroes and Asians. He had, however, always attributed such conduct to the bad attitudes of individuals. Now in South Africa he found color prejudice institutionalized and embodied in the law. In Natal and the Transvaal, he learned, no Indian could walk on the street after 9 P.M. without a government-issued pass. In the Orange Free State, Indians could neither own land nor engage in trade. In the Transvaal and the Orange Free State, both under Boer (Dutch) control, they were forced into ghettos and taxed three pounds each for residence permits. Everywhere, regardless of their caste, they were called "coolies" or "sammies."

Wearing his best turban and an expensive frock coat, Gandhi boarded a first-class coach in Durban for the five-day trip to Pretoria. At nine that night the train stopped at Maritzburg, the capital of Natal. A white man entered the compartment, was obviously startled to see a "colored" there, and left immediately. A few minutes later he returned, accompanied by two railway officials.

"Come along," one of the officials said to Gandhi. "You'll have to go to the baggage car where you belong."

"But I have a first-class ticket."

"No matter. You cannot remain in this compartment."

Indignant, Gandhi stayed where he was. "I was permitted to travel in this compartment in Durban and I insist on going on in it."

"No, you won't," said the official firmly. "If you don't leave I shall have to call a constable."

"I refuse to go voluntarily."

A policeman came, pulled Gandhi to his feet, and unceremoniously deposited him, with his luggage, on the station platform. A moment thereafter, the train steamed away. Trembling with rage, Gandhi picked up his handbag, leaving his heavier luggage in charge of the authorities, and took a seat in the unlit waiting room.

Maritzburg is a mountain town. It was winter and the

night was bitter cold. His overcoat was in one of the bags being held by the stationmaster. He did not dare ask for it, lest he be insulted again. So he sat through the night, shivering, trying to control his emotions as he sorted out his thoughts. A passenger came in about midnight and made a friendly effort to draw him into conversation. But Gandhi was obviously in no mood to talk and the passenger obligingly left him alone.

What should he do? Go back to India immediately? Stay and fight for his rights? Or forget about the insults, as Indians in South Africa were expected to do, go on to Pretoria, and return to India, as planned, a year from now when the

Maritzburg, Natal. It was here that Gandhi had his first personal experience of racial prejudice in South Africa.

case was settled? Deeply troubled, he was not even sure that he was asking himself the right questions.

Nobody knows quite what happened to him that night in Maritzburg. One can only know for certain that he was in a state of crisis and that he came out of it surer, calmer, wiser, and much, much older. He had come to South Africa because he had found conditions in Kathiawar intolerable. What sense did it make to go back because he had found conditions in South Africa even worse? To go home now, he decided, would be worse than defaulting on an obligation. It would be worse than cowardice, worse than defeat. It would be spiritual suicide. Thus, at some moment between midnight and dawn, Mohandas Gandhi learned that he could live in the world only if he committed himself to a lifelong effort to reform it. That was the kind of man he was, and in this agonizing act of self-discovery, he made his first giant step toward self-fulfillment.

The next day he resumed his journey to Pretoria. Around the issue of segregation he began to organize his future.

At Charlestown he had to transfer to a stagecoach for the overnight journey to Johannesburg. Though he had a coach ticket, the "leader," as the white man in charge was called, refused to let him sit with the other passengers. He was ordered to sit outside, next to the driver.

Some hours later, when the coach stopped at Pardekoph, the leader, in need of fresh air and a smoke, wanted Gandhi's seat. He spread a piece of dirty sackcloth on the footboard. "Here, sammy, you sit on this."

Gandhi said softly that he would move only if he could move to the coach seat that he had paid for. At that, the white man seized him by the arm and tried to drag him down. Gandhi grabbed the brass rails of the coachbox and clung to them, determined to keep his hold even at the risk of broken wristbones. Maddened at such impertinence, the leader swore and began beating him with his fists, stopping only when the coach passengers intervened. Still angry, he whispered a threat to "get" Gandhi once the coach reached Sanderton.

Fortunately, some Indian friends of Abdulla's were waiting to receive him at Sanderton. He spent the night with them, listening to stories of their daily indignities. Next morning, they escorted him to the station and stayed with him until they were sure he had found satisfactory accommodations on a different coach.

He got off at Pretoria, expecting to be welcomed by one of Abdulla's attorneys. He waited. No one came to meet him. He asked the ticket agent for the name of a hotel where he might be accepted. The agent was polite but of no help. Finally, an American Negro, recognizing his plight, took him to Johnston's Family Hotel. Mr. Johnston, a white American, offered to put Gandhi up for the night if he promised not to eat in the dining room. Gandhi agreed and went to his room to await dinner. His body was sore and bruised from the beating. He was lonely, tired, and sad. Mr. Johnston then made one of those simple, surprising gestures by which decent individuals regularly redeem the human race. He came to Gandhi, saying he was ashamed of himself, and invited him downstairs to join the other guests in the dining room.

One of the first things Gandhi learned after arriving in Pretoria was that the head of the Indian community was Abdulla's cousin and rival—Tyeb Sheth Haji Khan Muhammad. No public movement could possibly get under way without his support.

Gandhi called on Tyeb Sheth, expecting to be turned away as soon as he introduced himself as Abdulla's agent. Hurriedly, he explained that he meant to study the conditions of Indians in the Transvaal and that during his stay in Pretoria he wanted to become acquainted with every Indian living there. Would Tyeb Sheth help him? Gratifyingly, the merchant said he would and moved immediately to convene a meeting of all Indians in the city.

Thus, less than ten days after Maritzburg, Gandhi was on his feet, making his first public speech. Miraculously, he was poised, coherent if not eloquent. It was time, he said, for Indians to organize and make their grievances known to the authorities. Would they help him document their case? His audience responded enthusiastically.

The year in Pretoria was undoubtedly one of the most important in his life, for it was here that he began his po-

A formal portrait early in his South African period.

litical apprenticeship. He developed a small and grateful following, in part because he offered to teach English free to any Indian who wanted to learn. He pressed charges against the railway and won a modest concession: first and second-class tickets would be sold to Indians provided they appeared "well-dressed." He made a friend of the British Agent and obtained access to government reports of discriminatory practices throughout South Africa. His findings, reported periodically at meetings called by Tyeb Sheth, gave the Indian community a sense of solidarity it had never had before.

It was in Pretoria, too, that he turned into a skilled and confident lawyer. He was assigned to prepare the brief for Abdulla's attorney, not to argue the case. He had a chance to learn for himself what his teachers in London had tried vainly to tell him—that the test of a good lawyer is not his forensic ability in the courtroom but his competence at marshalling evidence.

It was a complicated case. The longer it remained unresolved, the more likely it appeared that both parties would be ruined by the mounting legal expenses. Gandhi, very much the junior employee, took it on himself to propose to Tyeb Sheth that he submit to arbitration. This was arranged, and the suit was subsequently settled out of court. Another problem immediately presented itself, however. The arbitration order required Tyeb to pay Abdulla 37,000 pounds in damages, plus costs. Were he to pay the whole amount at once, it would have left him no alternative but to declare bankruptcy, an action that in the unwritten code of Porbandar Moslems was considered worse than death. Distressed, Gandhi went to Abdulla and pleaded with him to allow his rival to pay in installments. With some reluctance, Abdulla agreed.

Thus, at twenty-five, Gandhi had pulled off his first "joyous compromise" and found his mark as a lawyer. "I had learned . . . that the true function of a lawyer is to unite parties riven asunder."

SEVEN

The Protest in South Africa

Grateful, Abdulla gave Gandhi a farewell party, an all-day affair to which virtually every Indian merchant in Durban was invited.

It so happened that on the day of the party the *Natal Mercury* carried an account of a bill, then pending in the Natal legislature, which would deprive all Indian settlers of their right to vote. When Gandhi commented indignantly that, if passed, the bill would constitute the "first nail in our coffin," it occurred to almost everybody at once that the guest of honor was the logical person to lead the fight to defeat it. Excited by the challenge, Gandhi agreed to postpone his return to India for thirty days.

He didn't know it, but he had made the decision that would keep him in South Africa for the next twenty years.

In all of Natal there were no more than two hundred and fifty Indians who had enough property to qualify as registered voters—hardly enough to threaten the power of the ten thousand eligible Europeans. But because the disfranchisement bill was so bald in asserting racial discrimination as a policy of state, it exposed the true intent behind a growing number of other repressive acts. That intent, plainly, was to make living conditions so intolerable for Indians in South

Africa that they would be forced either to leave the country or to accept the status of slaves.

Ironically, it was the abolition of slavery in the British colonies in 1833 that first brought Indians to South Africa. No longer able to force Africans to work in the mines or on the plantations, the white settlers began to import unemployed Indians, mostly from the congested districts of Madras and Bengal, as indentured laborers under five-year contracts. The Indians were promised free passage, board and lodging, and a wage of ten shillings (about $2.40) a month for the first year. The usual contract specified that at the end of five years the laborer could either renew his indenture or go back to India with all expenses paid.

So attracted, more than forty thousand Indians migrated to South Africa between 1860 and 1890. While most of them were employed in Natal, thousands came under indenture to white bosses in the Cape of Good Hope Colony, the Transvaal, and the Orange Free State; some even went to work in Zululand. Once released from their five-year terms, many of them chose the uncertainty of freedom in South Africa to the certainty of poverty in their home country. They bought small plots of land and gradually became self-supporting farmers. Meanwhile, into the cities of South Africa came thousands of free Indians—merchants, clerks, peddlers, artisans, and professional men—all, it seemed, with a special gift for earning pennies and saving dollars.

Before long, whether from fear that the Indians might lead the Negroes into revolt or whether merely from resentment of the Indians because of their growing affluence, the Europeans moved to put brown men into the same box with black men. Through a series of increasingly restrictive acts, the provincial legislatures made it virtually impossible for Indians to obtain business licenses and almost succeeded in banning free Indians from entering the country. By custom, and sometimes by law, Indians were forbidden to use many public facilities, including the sidewalks. If, as they tried to make their way down crowded streets they brushed against white pedestrians, they could expect to be pushed, kicked, or spat upon. (Gandhi was once kicked by a white policeman while walking in Pretoria.)

For thirty years Indians in South Africa had endured such oppression. Now, under Gandhi, they were being organized to protest for the first time.

To mount a campaign against the bill to repeal voting rights, he had precious little time. He set to work like a man inspired. Within twenty-four hours he had drafted and duplicated a statement of opposition, to which Abdulla's friends managed to affix five hundred signatures.

It had the effect of delaying the bill's passage by two days.

Undeterred, Gandhi's committee decided to appeal directly to Great Britain. For this purpose, he drafted a new petition. He worked fast but meticulously, supporting his argument with some precisely documented facts about the English laws of suffrage. During the next fortnight, his volunteers traveled to every village in the province, collecting signatures, and when the petition went to the Secretary of State for the Colonies, it bore the names of ten thousand of Natal's fifty thousand Indians. A thousand copies were printed and sent by post to every major newspaper in the British Empire. As a result, what had been ignored as a subject of purely colonial interest suddenly became an international issue. Both the *London Times* and the *Times of India* came out in favor of the committee's claims. Later, the Indian National Congress was to do the same. There was realistic hope that the bill would be vetoed.

Gandhi's month was up. But as long as the petition was still being reviewed in London there was plainly a need to maintain the sort of public pressure that he had so impressively created. Furthermore, by now it was clear to Durban's Indian merchants that their trading rights were inextricably linked to their political rights. The fight to protect and extend those rights in the face of hostile white control was going to be a long one. They needed Gandhi.

To keep him in South Africa, twenty merchants promised to give him enough legal work to guarantee him an income. He stayed.

The London Colonial Office vetoed the disfranchisement bill on the grounds that one part of the empire could not discriminate against citizens of another part. Gandhi's satisfaction, however, was short-lived. For merely by changing a few words the Natal Assembly brought the bill within the letter of the London ruling. It dropped the specific references to Indians and substituted "natives of countries which have not hitherto possessed elective representative institutions." In spirit, the amendment was not unlike the famous Grandfather Clause that North Carolina and Alabama used to bar American Negroes from the polls after Reconstruction.

Though disappointed by the unfavorable response of the Natal legislature, the Moslem merchants of Durban were enormously encouraged at having been able to get their case heard in London. Besides the new sense of pride in themselves, the experience left them with an unqualified

Durban, Natal, around the time Gandhi lived there. It was here that he founded the Natal Indian Congress.

admiration for the twenty-five-year-old Gandhi. They had never seen a man work so hard or so unselfishly. Prophetically, his earliest followers said they loved him even if they didn't understand him.

At Abdulla's urging, Gandhi called a public meeting on May 22 and founded the Natal India Congress. Though the name was inspired by the Indian National Congress, he conceived it only partly as a pressure group. In his mind it was also to be a mutual protective association, an agency for moral uplift, and a training school. Its activities were essentially political, but it could hardly function as a political party; by law of the ruling white minority, its members could neither vote nor hold public office. A U.S. counterpart would be the Mississippi chapter, say, of the National Association for the Advancement of Colored People as it was obliged to operate before World War II.

Indefatigable, Secretary Gandhi recruited new members and coached them in parliamentary procedure. He wrote the minutes as well as the policy statements. He collected the dues, kept the books, and ran the duplicating machine. He developed some ingenious fund-raising techniques. He soon learned that most merchants in a village pegged the amount of their own donations to the amount given by the leading merchant. Therefore, in much the fashion of one of today's Community Fund solicitors, he made it a habit to see the leading merchant first and to present him with a predetermined "fair-share" figure.

Once in the small village of Tongaat, such a merchant cordially invited Gandhi and his co-workers to dine with him but adamantly refused to pay the six pounds a month that Gandhi had him down for. Gandhi, however, knew his man. He knew, among other things, that out of courtesy the merchant would not eat unless his guests joined him. So Gandhi and his aides simply refused to eat until the merchant gave in. At dawn, just as it began to look as if the group had settled down to an undeclared fast, the merchant yielded, paid the six pounds, and ordered his servants to bring in the food. Well-to-do Indians as far as Stanger on the north coast and Charlestown in the interior soon got the message.

Gandhi became a skilled publicist. Between 1894 and 1898 the *London Times* ran eight feature stories on the Indian-Afrikaner problem, almost entirely in response to the interest he generated. But perhaps nothing pleased him more than the discovery that now he could make impromptu speeches. Intent on saying what he believed, and moved alternately by enthusiasm and indignation, he shed his old self-consciousness, almost without knowing it. Though his voice remained thin and uncommanding, his Indian audiences found his sincerity well-nigh irresistible. He spent a great deal of his time addressing village meetings.

He was a critic of his fellow Indians as well as their champion. To earn the respect of the British, he said, Indians must make themselves more respectable. He was constantly exhorting them to dress more neatly, practice better sanitation, behave more politely, work together, and be more ethical in their business conduct. It was a theme—self-help and cooperation— he was to orchestrate throughout his life.

But a complementary theme, devised as an appeal to the Europeans, he soon dropped. In his early days as a propaganadist, it was his custom to call on prominent Afrikaners and try to convince them that, contrary to the prevalent opinion among whites, Indians were law-abiding, thrifty, industrious, and generally of good character. He stopped after the head of the Transvaal Asiatic Department, having heard him out, said: "Mr. Gandhi, you are preaching to the converted. It is not the vices of the Indians that Europeans in this country fear. It is their virtues."

Late in 1896 he returned to India to fetch Kasturbai and the children. The six-month visit proved especially instructive. It taught him that the hazards of public service are sometimes greater than the rewards; that both are excessive and ego-threatening; and that, in the interest of survival and sanity, every politician has to work out his own way of coping with them. Typically, Gandhi found it easier to handle the hazards than the rewards.

In his case, the rewards came first. On the eve of his departure Abdulla and his friends showered him with expensive gifts. Arriving in Bombay, he was warmly received by leaders of all the important political factions, to whom he had become the symbol of Indian suffering overseas. In Madras, the district from which so many indentured laborers had been recruited, he was given a hero's welcome. Two British-owned newspapers interviewed him sympathetically.

In Rajkot, he spent a month writing a pamphlet, "a purposely subdued picture" of conditions in South Africa. It sold nearly twenty thousand copies, was widely quoted, and made him even more popular. Except in South Africa.

A four-line cable from Reuter's, headlined in the Natal newspapers, made him the most hated man in the colony. "A pamphlet published in London," reported the *Mercury*, "declares that Indians in Natal are robbed and assaulted and treated like beasts." The effect was to give Gandhi's political enemies in Durban more ammunition than they needed. They accused him of "smearing the country that had harbored him," of "dragging Europeans . . . in the gutter and painting them as black as his own skin." They charged him in particular with having organized an agency to flood the colony with Indian immigrants.

This last charge was based on a news report that his boat had set sail from Bombay at the same time as another one, the two of them carrying about eight hundred Indians. The whites in Durban refused to believe it a mere coincidence. Incensed, two thousand of them met in the Durban town hall and demanded that the government send the "free Indians" back where they came from. By the time they dropped anchor, the situation was so tense that the two ships had to be quarantined for three weeks.

When the passengers were finally allowed to disembark, Gandhi arranged for Kasturbai and the children to get off safely in the company of friends. He followed a few hours later, but he had hardly descended the gangplank when he was set upon by a mob, chased down a street, and struck with rotten eggs, stones, and bricks. Beaten and kicked, his turban torn from his head, he almost fainted with pain. He was at the point of collapse when the wife of the police superintendent came on the scene. She opened her parasol to shield him from the brickbats and stayed with him until the police arrived.

Escorted to the home of a friend, he hardly had time to dress his wounds when another mob formed and surrounded the house. From a darkened room, he heard them sing, "We'll hang old Gandhi on the sour apple tree." They threatened to burn down the property if he did not surrender. To save him, the police superintendent sent two detectives into the house. Gandhi put on the uniform of an Indian constable, with a Madrasi scarf wrapped around a plate to resemble a helmet. The detectives put on the costumes of Indian merchants. Thus disguised, they slipped out of the back of the house, into a lane leading to a neighborhood shop, through the shop onto a side street, and from there to the police station. Gandhi stayed in the station three days, until tempers in the town had cooled enough for him to leave.

He had to do something, his friends said. Gandhi agreed. What he did, however, was scarcely what they had in mind. Whether by inspiration or by design, he proceeded to mix what was to become his standard formula for dealing with the enemy: truth with forgiveness. He gave an interview to a reporter for the *Natal Advertiser,* during which he refuted the charges leveled against him. He gave the reporter copies of all the speeches he had made in India, as well as a copy of the controversial pamphlet. The *Advertiser* not only published the interview but carried an editorial condemning the mob.

In London, the Secretary of State for the Colonies cabled Natal with instructions that Gandhi's assailants be prosecuted. Gandhi, however, refused to press charges. He explained that it was a principle with him not to seek redress for a personal wrong. Besides, his attackers had not been so much at fault as the government officials whose irresponsible charges had inflamed them. Shamed, the European community gave him its grudging respect.

Throughout this period, and for some years to come, Gandhi held that Indian independence and unity could be achieved only within the Empire. Therefore, when the Boer War broke out in 1899, he had little difficulty in deciding where his duty lay.

Some leading members of the Natal Indian Congress did not agree. They disliked the English as much as they did the Boers and pressed for a policy of neutrality. The Boers were stronger and likely to win, they argued, so why do something that might invite reprisals when the war was over? Gandhi called this cowardice. Certainly Indians in Natal had been denied elementary rights, but he maintained that merely to claim rights was to accept some corresponding obligations. He won the debate.

By way of demonstrating Indian loyalty to the Crown, he volunteered to organize an ambulance corps. The Natal

British soldiers, freshly arrived, set up camp shortly after the outbreak of the Boer War.

government first spurned the offer, insisting that the Indians would be more bother than help. But as the war wore on and the Boers were advancing, the government changed its mind. Under Gandhi's leadership, eleven hundred Indians were recruited—three hundred free Indians and about eight hundred indentured laborers furloughed by their masters. Trained as nurses and stretcher-bearers, they were sent to the front almost immediately. Their job was to receive the wounded just outside the firing line and carry them, sometimes as far as twenty miles, to the nearest base.

During the bloody fighting at Spio Kop, Gandhi and his men went onto the battlefield and worked under fire without letup for three weeks. Sometime during that engagement, a British editor came across Gandhi sitting by the roadside eating a regulation army biscuit. Gandhi was sporting a drooping black mustache. He wore a khaki uniform, a broad-brimmed felt hat, and a Red Cross armband. "Every man in Buller's force was dull and depressed," the correspondent wrote, "and d___tion was invoked on everything. But Gandhi was stoical in his bearing, cheerful, and confident in his conversations, and had a jaunty eye." When the corps was disbanded, Gandhi and thirty-six of his colleagues won war medals. His men were praised as "Sons of the Empire" in the British press. Among those who made a point of complimenting him on his return to Durban were the ringleaders of the mob that had tried to lynch him.

EIGHT

The Transformation

According to Gandhi's recollections, the years from 1894 to 1900 were "a period of half-baked knowledge . . . indulgence and inexperience." He dates the beginning of what he calls his "transformation" from 1900. By that time, one gathers, he had come to the settled belief that truth is power and renunciation the way to truth. For the next six years, he moved deliberately, almost by plan, to simplify his life—to strip himself to a loincloth, literally. At the same time, he sought a way to organize his convictions into a form that others would understand and respond to. The transformation, he implies, was completed in 1906. That was the year he became a celibate. That was the year that his intensely personal philosophy became one with a strategy of protest for the masses.

But whether it actually happened this way is open to question. It is true that, through an absolutely incredible exercise in self-control, Gandhi found the courage to act as he believed. It is no less true that he consciously, positively, and methodically thought through the elements of a coherent personal ethic. That he was then able to convert this personal ethic into a workable political method is not only true but an event of enduring historical significance.

But Gandhi's transformation did not follow the straight line that his autobiography implies. Despite its several recognizable crises, the process cannot be divided neatly into beginning, middle, and end. One has, for instance, only to examine his behavior with a half-critical eye to recognize signs of change long before 1900. Indeed, if we are to understand the Gandhian ethic as it was later to be mobilized for the independence of India, we must now try to see Gandhi plain as he lived and grew from 1894 to 1906. We start with two propositions:

1. For much of this time he was in a state of psychological tension. He wanted to be an activist in the world of men, power, and politics; with equal fervor he wanted to be an ascetic in the world of nature. He was torn between his obligation to confront evil and an instinct to retreat from it. He lived like a man of wealth even though he identified with the poor and the dispossessed. He loved Kasturbai but often had reason to hate himself for his behavior toward her. Though he loved India, there were times when he felt as if India had rejected him; he could not think of returning without tasting the memory of his failure. His values were neither Indian nor European but somewhere in-between. He hoped for approval of the English authorities even as he was in the act of defying them.

2. Through his "transformation" Gandhi outgrew some of his internal conflicts and learned to live with the others. But there was a part of him that remained unaltered by his transformation, that could never be explained or contained by the logic of his philosophy. That was his essential *humanness*—an interest in people that bordered on meddling; a happy facility for compromise, even at the risk of confounding his friends more than his enemies; a habit of reading into books and people whatever he found pleasing and forgetting what he did not; an irresistible, and irrational, optimism; a playful sense of humor; above all, a flair for doing the unexpected. It added up to a unique kind of magic, and though it eludes precise definition it was as important to his leadership as his integrity, intelligence, and willpower.

65

Without it, Mohandas would probably have never become Mahatma.

Almost as a condition for staying in South Africa, Gandhi had asked Abdulla to guarantee him enough in legal fees to live "in a style usual for barristers." It was obligatory, he said, that his home be a credit to the Indian community.

With the promise of three hundred pounds ($1500) a year, he rented an impressive English-style house on the beach. He hired a cook and a house servant and, inviting some law clerks and a few Indian friends to come live with him, set up his household carefully as a model of the Hindu family. He was, by today's political standards, acutely image-conscious. Both to enhance his prestige and to broaden his acquaintanceship with the influential citizens of Durban, he began to entertain regularly, serving as many delicacies as he could within the limits of his spiceless diet.

He became the first "colored" barrister to be admitted as an advocate to the Supreme Court of Natal, despite objections from the all-white Natal Law Society. In time he built up a remarkably good practice. He earned as much as six thousand pounds ($30,000) a year, mostly in arbitration fees. A famous picture of the period shows him with his secretary and three clerks, seated in front of an office window on which is imprinted, "M. K. Gandhi, Attorney." He is wearing a suit of fashionable English cut, a white shirt with a stiff white detachable collar, a dark necktie, and brightly polished shoes.

One day, an untouchable, "a Tamil man in tattered clothes, headgear in hand, two front teeth broken and mouth bleeding," came to his office, trembling and weeping. The "headgear" was a native scarf, and the man held it before him in an attitude of obeisance. By rigidly enforced custom, no indentured laborer could appear in the presence of a European without first removing his headpiece. On meeting Gandhi, the man had automatically taken off his scarf as if he, Gandhi, were a European. Gandhi winced. Softly but firmly, he told the man to put his scarf back on his head and keep it there.

66

The successful lawyer (center) poses with his office staff in Durban, South Africa. The days of storm and controversy still lay ahead.

Between sobs, the serf told Gandhi that he had been beaten by his master, a well-known resident of Durban. Gandhi took him to a doctor, then, armed with a medical affidavit, called on his master. Speaking quietly, he managed to cut through the Englishman's anger, telling him that charges would not be pressed if he would agree to release the worker. The Englishman agreed, whereupon Gandhi quickly arranged for the man's indenture to be transferred to someone less sadistic. After that, he became known all over the country as the champion of the Indian poor. "A

67

regular stream of indentured laborers began to pour into my office." Gradually he began to build a file of human grievances against the indenture system as convincing as his steadily expanding legal argument.

It was during these same trial-and-error years that his "natural aptitude for nursing developed into passion." On his 1896 visit to India he learned that a brother-in-law was seriously ill in Bombay. He arranged to have him brought to the family home in Rajkot and there attended him faithfully until his death many weeks later. When plague broke out during that same visit, he volunteered his services to the Rajkot prince and was named to an emergency sanitation committee. The committee's assignment was to inspect all the latrines in town and to clean those that constituted threats to the public health. Typically, he went into the quarters of the untouchables, where other committee members refused to go, as readily as he did to those of the upper classes.

Back in Durban, it became his unfailing routine to put in two hours every morning as a nurse in a Christian mission. With increasing frequency, the lame and the diseased, including lepers, came to his home for shelter. He would dress their wounds, feed them, and sometimes nurse them for days before taking them to a government hospital.

His fondness for nursing could not be explained easily. He was moved, undoubtedly, by tenderness and the desire to be of service. But on occasion, it seemed, his interest in serving the helpless got confused with some particular need to do for those who were perfectly able to help themselves. It was as if he went out of his way to do the nastiest, hardest, most degrading jobs, all for the purpose of testing himself, to see if he *could* do them and be happy doing them. "Service which is rendered without joy helps neither the servant nor the served," he would say.

Kasturbai could understand his interest in the sick and, although she wished they didn't demand quite so much of his time, willingly helped him take care of them. But what she could not understand was why her husband insisted that he and she clean the chamber pots in the rooms occupied by their several roomers. In proper Indian homes, this was a chore assigned to the "sweeper" or to an untouchable, and why her husband refused to employ one for that purpose was beyond her comprehension. That he cleaned the pots himself was bad enough; that he made her do it, too, was even worse; that he not only made her empty the pots but told her she had to be cheerful about it was just too much.

An orthodox Hindu, Kasturbai particularly resented having to do such menial tasks for one of the law clerks, a former untouchable who had become a Christian. She scolded, fussed, sulked, wept, and pleaded, but Gandhi was unyielding. He was the husband, he gave the orders; she was the wife, she took them. That was the fixed relationship in an Indian family. She had no choice but to obey. Besides, he told her, it was part of her education and it was his duty to educate her. She obeyed him, but he could neither force her to like it nor stop her from complaining about it. Gandhi got more and more out of sorts with her.

One day he spied her descending the stairs, holding a chamber pot as if it were something evil and sinister. Her eyes were swollen and red from crying.

Suddenly he had had enough. "I will not stand this nonsense in my house!" he screamed.

"Then *keep* your house," Kasturbai replied with spirit. "Keep your house to yourself and let me go!"

He grabbed her by the hand and dragged her to the gate, meaning to push her into the street. He was beside himself with anger. Kasturbai began to sob as if abandoned. "Must you so far forget yourself?" she asked, holding back. "Where am I to go? For Heaven's sake, behave yourself and shut the gate. Let us not be found making scenes like this!"

Her tears shamed him. Shaken, he closed the gate, appalled at the violence that had seized him. Once again he was reminded that he had much to learn about himself.

Kasturbai sometimes found his "do-it-yourself" notions almost as trying as his insistence on doing for others. When a white barber in Pretoria refused to cut his hair, he learned to cut his own, and did so the rest of his life. In Durban, where washermen failed to come up to his meticulous standards, he bought a book on garment care and taught himself how to wash, starch, and press his own shirts. In 1897, shortly before the birth of his third son, Ramdas, he read *Advice to a Mother*. From that time on he took care of the babies. He actually delivered his fourth child, Devadas, born in 1900.

As a matter of principle, he refused to send his sons to a school for European children, even though his status as a lawyer would have made them eligible. For a while he employed an English governess but let her go when it became clear that she would never be able to teach the children their mother tongue. After that he taught the boys himself.

Keeping fit, he was convinced, was mostly a matter of daily exercise and a sparse, vegetarian diet. He took long walks every day, frequently as long as ten miles, at a pace that was just short of a dogtrot. There were few disorders, including wounds, that in his opinion could not be cured by a combination of fasting, hot water, and mud packs. According to his own testimony, he once cured himself of persistent headaches simply by doing without breakfast. His autobiography also records incidents of curing Kasturbai of persistent bleeding by putting her on a salt-free seedless diet; of breaking the fever of ten-year-old Manilal by wrapping him in wet sheet packs; and of healing eight-year-old Ramdas' broken arm with dressings of clean earth. On at least two occasions he kept members of his family on strict vegetarian diets even though medical doctors warned him that their lives depended on their getting beef and chicken broth. The fact that they rallied under his home ministrations "added somewhat to my reputation as a quack."

By 1900 it was clear that his experiments in the kitchen and the sickroom were no passing fancies but a sincere, if sometimes willful, manifestation of a lifelong search for the balance between flesh and spirit. Kasturbai resigned herself

With Kasturbai on their return to India from South Africa in 1901; their marriage was to last sixty-two years.

to the fact that her husband-teacher was also a perennial student.

In South Africa, Gandhi was a sought-after lawyer and a respected political leader. In India he was a self-conscious, awkward apprentice, a bit too innocent for his own good.

Although by most outward signs his 1896 trip was a great success, his ego was under constant assault. India was the land of his birth, yet most of it was strange country to him, and what wasn't strange was scarred with painful memories of adolescent hurts and of his early failures as an attorney. As exhilarated as he was by the attention accorded him by India's native political leaders, he usually found himself awed and tongue-tied in their presence. The poise that he had developed before audiences in Natal completely abandoned him on the platform in Bombay. When he rose to face his audience, he trembled so with fear that he could hardly speak above a whisper. Humiliated, he had to turn over his text to a local orator.

Generally, his work in South Africa was commended by the Indian leaders he most admired. Occasionally, though, he would be told bluntly that he ought to be working in his own country and he would be momentarily overwhelmed with guilt. "Is there lack of work here?" he was asked peevishly by a high court official. "Our people in South Africa are no doubt in difficulty, but . . . let us win self-government here and we shall automatically help our countrymen there."

The official was right. Eventually, Gandhi knew, the war for freedom and dignity would have to be won on home ground. But he was not then ready to return to India. In South Africa, as secretary of the Natal Indian Congress, he had a personal laboratory in political organization, a chance to shape a movement in his own image. To enter Indian politics prematurely would mean, at best, a long and risky period as a junior aide to the least objectionable leader of one of the many bickering factions. That wouldn't do. When he returned, he meant to be recognized as a leader in his own right.

By 1901, he was willing to take the risk. For the moment the British victory over the Boers promised an early redress of the main Indian grievances. His record was by then so well known that several prominent politicians in Bombay were encouraging him to join them. In addition, he feared that if he stayed much longer in South Africa his "main business might become merely money-making."

He did not find it easy to leave Natal. To the Indian community he had made himself the indispensable man, so much so that its leaders made him promise that he would come back if within a year they felt the situation required him. They gave him going-away presents so valuable and in such volume as to pose a ticklish dilemma. For the past several years he had been trying deliberately to simplify his life and that of his family, whether they liked it or not. He had, in particular, been exhorting practically everybody within earshot to conquer the infatuation with jewelry. What, then, was he now to do with this small fortune in pearls, diamonds, rubies, gold and silver—among them a fifty-guinea gold necklace intended for his wife?

He spent a sleepless night, torn between his concerns for financial security, which he would surely have were he to keep the jewels, and personal freedom, some degree of which he knew would be forfeited if he did not give them back. By dawn he had made up his mind; the kind of freedom he sought could only be achieved by ridding himself of property, not in acquiring more. Over Kasturbai's vehement protest, he transferred all the jewels to a Durban bank, using them as security to set up a trust fund for the needy.

Shortly after his arrival in India, he went to Calcutta to attend his first meeting of the All-India National Congress. The experience was an eye-opener. He had asked for the privilege of introducing a resolution for support of Indian rights in South Africa and had been enormously pleased when Sir Pherozeshah Mehta advised him that his motion would be entertained. But he was given only five minutes to present his case and, rattled, he mistook the warning bell for a signal that his time was up. He sat down in mid-sentence. It didn't matter. It turned out that all resolutions, heard or unheard, understood or not, passed unanimously.

To Gandhi, the Congress was a distressing example of the general national disunity. The problems of caste and untouchability were everywhere. "To the Tamil delegates, even the sight of others while they were dining meant pollution, so a special room had to be made for them . . . It was a kitchen, dining room, washroom all in one." Onto these prevailing differences, party members superimposed their own pecking order. The leaders were quartered in private camps where they lived like princes, each with his own retinue. Those of the lower orders were divided almost evenly between delegates and volunteers. Presumably, the volunteers were to do all the work, on orders from the delegates. The volunteers, however, had a habit of delegating work to other volunteers and, as a consequence, most of their energies were spent in passing the buck. Even when a delegate or volunteer was willing to work, he was handicapped by the simple fact that nobody could tell him what to do. Except for the small cadre at the top, the whole Congress seemed to be suffering from chronic inexperience. And no wonder: "The Congress would meet three days a year and then go to sleep."

Far from being disheartened by all this, Gandhi reacted as if challenged. Part of the challenge, he decided, would be to introduce to the Indian National Congress some of the simple, elementary techniques of organization that he had worked out for the Natal Indian Congress. That, however, would take time and the careful cultivation of party members. Before he could expect to influence them, he would have to serve them; before he could be their teacher, he would have to be their student. So throughout the meeting he busied himself cleaning latrines ("I found no one to share the honor of doing it"), serving as clerk and bearer to one of the Congress secretaries, and seeking out interviews with the more important delegates.

His zeal brought a conspicuous reward. The great leader of Indian nationalism, G. K. Gokhale, decided to make him his protégé.

For a month after the Congress adjourned, Gandhi was a guest in Gokhale's Calcutta home, which also served as the intelligence center for the party's moderate wing. Gokhale introduced him to important visitors, sent him on confidential errands to important offices, and in general gave him a splendid baptism into provincial politics. Whenever Gandhi appeared to be more observer than participant, the aristocratic, 35-year-old statesman would push him into interviews with prominent party functionaries. "This sort of reserve will not do," he said gently after one meeting during which Gandhi had been too awed to speak. "I want you to do Congress work and for that you must get in touch with as many people as possible." Very quickly, the two settled into an older-and-younger brother relationship. Observing the great man at work, Gandhi could find only two flaws worth noting: he insisted on traveling in his own carriage, refusing to ride in the public tram, and he *never* took any exercise.

When his month in Calcutta was up, he decided to travel to Rajkot in an unheated third-class coach, the better to acquaint himself with the hardships of the poor. It was a week-long journey and in those days third-class accommodations were hardly as comfortable as cattle cars and, if possible, even more crowded and dirty. To equip himself, he bought a canvas bag, a long woolen coat, a peasant-styled *dhoti* (loincloth), a towel and a shirt, a blanket, and a water jug.

Though Gokhale did not fully understand Gandhi's purpose in traveling third-class, he could not help admiring him for it. Gandhi, he knew, was not like other men, nor was he going to be like any other politician. Consummate politician that he was himself, Gokhale may have suspected what at the time even Gandhi only dimly perceived—that among the likes of these third-class passengers would be found a new constituency of revolutionary force. In any event, dressed in a silk turban and a jacket and *dhoti* of equally fine cloth, the great man drove to the station in his private carriage to see his protégé off. His *bon voyage* gift was a metal tiffin box filled with sweet balls and *puris,* fried bread.

In Rajkot, Gandhi settled down to law practice under the patronage of his old well-wisher, Kevalram Mavji Dave, the *vakil* who had induced him to go to England. Gokhale, however, kept entreating him to settle in Bombay where he could not only make a good living in the law but could also be active in party work. After a while, Kevalram Dave came, too, to believe that Gandhi's talents were being squandered in Rajkot. One day he came to Gandhi, saying "We will not suffer you to vegetate here. . . You are destined to do public work." Thus, after only a few months in his old home town, he moved with his family to Bombay, renting a fine bungalow in Santa Cruz.

For a while it looked as if his future were laid out for him. Then, suddenly, Gandhi received a cable from South Africa. "Chamberlain expected here. Please return immediately." Remembering his promise, Gandhi told Kasturbai and the children good-bye and immediately left for Durban. He meant to be gone, at most, a year.

Joseph Chamberlain, the British Colonial Secretary, had come to South Africa to do what he could to create an amicable spirit of accommodation between the victorious British and the defeated Boers. When, in Durban, he received Gandhi and the deputation of Indians, he was plainspoken and to the point. He could not afford to run the risk of aggravating the whites by championing a minority cause. "The Imperial Government has little control over self-governing colonies," he said. "You must try your best to placate the Europeans if you wish to live in their midst."

Disappointed, Gandhi followed Chamberlain to Johannesburg, where the Indians had asked him to present their case.

But there Gandhi could not even get an audience with the Secretary, being referred instead to the chief of a new and corrupt government bureau called the Asiatic Department. Shocked, he realized that far from being reversed by the British victory, anti-Indian practices had been given fresh license. The British had instructed a special committee to examine all laws in the former Boer states and to repeal those it found "inconsistent with the liberty of Queen Victoria's subjects." But, as if eager to pacify the defeated enemy, the committee had chosen to interpret "subject" as "white subject," thus neatly excluding Negroes, Chinese, and Indians from the reformed code.

Viewing the dismal situation, Gandhi decided he had no alternative but to stay and fight. And this time, he vowed,

Sir Joseph Chamberlain
was the first British Colonial Secretary sympathetic to the problems of the overseas colonies. Gandhi sought his help on the plight of the Indians in South Africa.

A model young professional in 1904, when this photo was taken, Gandhi adopted an ascetic Hindu lifestyle a year later and was rarely seen thereafter in Western dress.

he would not leave South Africa until the fight had been won.

Since Johannesburg was the stronghold of the Asiatic Department and the Asiatic Department was now clearly the enemy, it only made sense for him to set up base in Johannesburg. He therefore enrolled himself as an attorney in the Transvaal Supreme Court and, as quickly as he could, arranged for Kasturbai and the children to join him.

In 1904, he was persuaded to found a weekly newspaper, *Indian Opinion,* in partnership with two Indian journalists. Although to keep the publication afloat cost him almost all his savings, he considered it a good investment. At its peak the paper had a readership of 11,000, and through its columns he had an opportunity to express his views on everything from the virtues of unleavened bread to the evils of the indenture system.

Indian Opinion was published in Durban, twenty-four hours by rail from Johannesburg. Sometime late in 1904, as he was on his way there to take care of one of the recurrent financial crises, an English journalist named Henry Polak gave him a copy of *Unto This Last* by John Ruskin, suggesting that reading it might make the trip less tedious. Once he began the book, Gandhi could not put it down. He read it with mounting excitement and when he had finished he stayed awake through the night, thinking about it. By the time day broke, he had made up his mind: he would change his life "in accordance with the ideals of the book."

Ruskin, an English essayist, said many things in *Unto This Last,* mostly to do with the failure of the classical economists to treat money and work in human terms. Gandhi, who admittedly had a selective memory ("it was a habit with me to forget what I did not like and to carry out in practice what I liked"), found in it powerful confirmation of some of his own developing convictions. From *Unto This Last* he eagerly abstracted three principles.

1. The good of the individual is contained in the good of all;

2. Manual occupations are as valuable as intellectual ones; and

3. The life of the laborer—the man who works with his hands—is the only life worth living.

His way of testing Ruskin's ideas was to buy a hundred acres near Durban, transfer there the presses of *Indian Opinion*, and persuade as many of the workers as he could and all the cousins he had brought with him to South Africa to move there and help him establish a communal back-to-nature settlement. The farm was located thirteen miles from Durban and two and a half miles from the nearest station, Phoenix. The place had a few orange and mango trees, some other unidentifiable fruit trees, a dilapidated cottage, and a dangerous infestation of snakes. In time, eight buildings of corrugated iron were put up.

Although the Gandhis stayed at the Phoenix settlement off and on for the next ten years, it never became the place of retirement—the place where he could "find the joy of service" through manual labor—that he intended it to be. He was kept too busy in Johannesburg. Determined nevertheless to practice Ruskin's principles, he reorganized the Johannesburg household into an urban equivalent. Living with him now, besides his immediate family, were a number of relatives, a servant, an Englishwoman, and Mr. and Mrs. Henry Polak. (Utterly fascinated by Gandhi's ideas, Polak had quit his newspaper job, qualified as an articled clerk, and joined the Gandhi law firm.) Happily, the Polaks helped grind the flour by hand, using a heavy iron mill that Gandhi bought for seven pounds. Kasturbai and Mrs. Polak did all the kitchen work, while it was the children's job to keep the latrines clean. Gandhi and Polak walked to and from the office each day, a distance of about five miles. As often as he could, Gandhi would get the children to accompany him, instructing them in their day's lessons as they walked.

Service was now the dominant theme in his life. Once local officials tried to oust Indians from their land without compensation. Gandhi sued seventy times and won all but one case. Shortly thereafter, plague broke out in Johannesburg's Indian ghetto. Gandhi set up a hospital in an empty building, nursing the victims himself. When the authorities decided to set fire to the hovels in an effort to burn out the disease, the Indians agreed to move to a campsite near the city only when Gandhi told them to. They would obey nobody else.

But the truly significant drama of these years was not in the events of Johannesburg or Phoenix. The most important things about Gandhi were happening in his mind and heart, and they centered on an obsessive search for truth which, in his case, was synonymous with a search for identity.

A good part of this search led him into a comparative study of Buddhism, Christianity, Islam, and Hinduism. Sir Edwin Arnold's *Light of Asia* was one of his favorite books and Gautama the Buddha, its subject, one of his favorite spiritual heroes. With Christian friends he would sometimes argue that Gautama's compassion was superior to that of Jesus because "it was not confined to mankind but was extended to all living beings." In England he had been almost overwhelmed by the New Testament. Indeed, he later credited the inspiration for his basic philosophy of nonviolence to the Sermon on the Mount. For most of his years in South Africa he had strong and gratifying ties to the Quaker colony, which persistently tried to convert him and almost did. But Gandhi could not accept the idea that Jesus was the only incarnate son of God. "If God could have sons, all of us were his sons," he said. Also, the fact that Christians were so bent on converting the world implied a presumption of superiority that he found repulsive. "What have I to take the Assam hillsmen?" he once asked a missionary. "Rather than ask them to join my prayer, I would join their prayer." But what to him was most objectionable in Christianity, at least as it was popularly interpreted by the Protestants of his day, was the doctrine that faith could be separated from ethics. It seemed altogether too easy a religion in which sins could be redeemed merely by professing faith in Jesus.

He had been introduced to Islam several years before through Thomas Carlyle's essay on "The Hero as Prophet." Now, at Abdulla's urging, he read a translation of the Koran. He was struck by the courage with which Mahomet and his followers faced humiliation and hardship. But he saw nothing so different or so compelling in the Koran that he should abandon the Hinduism of his mother.

He did not accept every Hindu tenet. The oft-quoted text, "For women there can be no freedom," ascribed to Manu the Lawmaker, he regarded as an editor's error. If it were not, then he could only say that in Manu's time women did not receive the status they deserved. Also, he quarreled vigorously with those who supported untouchability with verses from the Vedas. "If untouchability could be a part of Hinduism," he wrote, "it could but be a rotten part or an excrescence."

Buddha, founder of the Buddhist religion, was one of Gandhi's spiritual heroes. Buddhism, which began in India, later spread to China, Japan, Tibet, Korea and other parts of Asia. Indian Buddhism was later reabsorbed by Hinduism.

Still, he always came back to Hinduism as the most personally satisfying religion. In Hinduism, he decided, "there is room for all the prophets of the world. . . Hinduism tells everyone to worship God according to his own faith . . . and so it lives at peace with all religions."

But more than any other single influence, it was *The Bhagavad-Gita* that gave Gandhi a philosophy for his transformation.

He rediscovered *The Gita* in 1903. He was at the time friendly with a group of Theosophists in Johannesburg and with them formed a sort of Seeker's Club for the reading and study of Hindu scriptures. As much to prepare for these meetings as to fill what he recognized as a gap in his education, he decided to commit to memory all seven hundred verses. He regularly allowed thirty-five minutes for his morning toilet—twenty minutes for the bath and fifteen for the toothbrush. It now became his habit to learn by heart at least one verse every morning as he brushed his teeth. On a wall opposite his washbasin he put up slips of paper on which he had written the verses. The fifteen minutes allowed him enough time to memorize the new lines and to recall the verses he had learned during the preceding week.

Essentially, *The Gita* is a long, profound, philosophical dialogue between Lord Krishna, the human embodiment of Vishnu, the supreme God, and Arjuna, the leader of one faction in an ancient civil war. It deals with the science and practice of yoga—that is, the union of the human soul with the universal spirit through the withdrawal of the senses from all external objects. Like all scripture, it is rich in metaphor and subject to different interpretations. Not surprisingly, Gandhi read it from his own highly individualistic point of view. He rejected the orthodox Hindu interpretation that sees it as a divine summons to kill as a caste obligation. To him *The Gita* was an allegory in which the battlefield was the soul and Arjuna a symbol of man's higher impulses struggling against evil. Now, as a result of deep introspection over numberless Johannesburg mornings, he reduced its message to a single thought. Truth was power and the way to power lay through desirelessness.

The words *aparigraha* (non-possession) and *samabajva* (equability) burned their way into his consciousness. "But how to cultivate and preserve that equability was the question. How was one to treat alike insulting, insolent, and corrupt officials, co-workers of yesterday raising meaningless opposition, and men who had always been good to one? How was one to divest oneself of all possessions? Was not the body itself possession enough? Were not wife and children possessions? Was I to destroy all the cupboards of books I had? Was I to give up all I had and follow Him? Straight came the answer: I could not follow Him unless I gave up all I had.

"The study of English law came to my help. Snell's discussion of the maxims of equity came to my memory. I understood more clearly, in the light of *The Gita* teaching, the implication of the word 'trustee.' . . . Those who desire salvation should act like trustees who, though having control of great possessions, regard not an iota of them as their own."

Many years later the Mahatma advised his followers: "Only give up a thing when you want some other condition so much that the thing no longer has any attraction for you, or when it seems to interfere with that which is more greatly desired." In 1903, the New Testament, the Koran, the *Gita*—most of all *The Gita*—were all enjoining him to give up property, sex, and family. But for what? Though the trend of his life was increasingly toward austerity he could not yet clearly answer for what.

The Gita had lasting impact. It also had some immediate results. He canceled his life insurance policy, convinced that God, "who created my wife and children as well as myself, would take care of them." And he wrote his brother, Laxmidas, in Rajkot, not to expect any more money from him, that henceforth all his earnings would go for the benefit of the community. When Laxmidas replied sternly that Mohan must support the family as his father had before him, Gandhi's rejoinder was that Laxmidas had only to expand the meaning of "family" to understand the wisdom and necessity of his action. Laxmidas could not agree. From that day until within a few months of his death, he would have nothing to do with his odd, "selfish and ungrateful" younger brother.

In May of 1906, Gandhi's routine was shattered by news of the Zulu Rebellion in Natal. Although the causes were vague, the British were mobilizing and Gandhi, who still considered himself a loyal subject of the Crown, promptly volunteered to organize an Indian Ambulance Corps.

Zulu warriors in their native surroundings. When the Zulus revolted against the British in 1906, Gandhi organized an Indian Ambulance Corps.

In Durban, Gandhi recruited twenty-four men, mostly former indentured servants from South India. On induction, the corps was assigned to a fast-moving column of mounted infantry and ordered to nurse wounded Zulus, a duty that white corpsmen had refused. The infantrymen were under orders to move on a moment's notice, to whatever native village was reported to be in a state of incipient revolt. Once camp was struck, Gandhi and his stretcher-bearers followed on foot.

For a good part of his six weeks' service, Gandhi was in motion, sometimes marching as much as forty miles a day. On these long, silent marches through the sparsely populated land Gandhi fell to thinking about the purpose of life, the senseless war that he was in, the meaning of renunciation, the nature of God, and his own future in South Africa. The marches usually led to some simple *Kraal of* "uncivilized" Zulus where the soldiers rarely met any resistance but invariably shot off their rifles anyway. The marches brought Gandhi to a turning point.

The rebellion, as he saw it, was a sham. There had indeed been a disturbance. A Zulu chief had resisted payment of a newly imposed tax and had speared a sergeant who had come to collect. The British had responded by magnifying a manhunt into a war of counter-revolution, the main casualties of which were innocent black villagers. Gandhi was appalled to discover that of the wounded in his charge not one had been hurt in battle. About half had been taken prisoner and flogged so badly they were left with festering sores; others were "friendlies" who, although given badges to distinguish them from the "enemy," had been shot by mistake. His respect for Europeans was not enhanced by the fact that white soldiers habitually stood on the other side of the fence that surrounded the nursing compound, alternately swearing at the suffering Zulus and urging the Indian medics to "let the savages die."

His experience brought home the horrors of war more vividly than anything he had seen during the Boer War. Violence, he decided irrevocably, was an insult to God's intent for man. He could ease his conscience only with the thought that if it had not been for him the Zulus would not have been cared for at all.

In the midst of these pitiful, frightened, and dying black men—in the employment of men who seemed to value life only if it came packaged in a white skin—Gandhi came to equate life with time and to see the acceptance of death as a condition of freedom.

A man's achievements in life, he reasoned, were nothing more than the constructive uses he made of his time on earth. With so much to do, and with time in such uncertain supply, he obviously could not afford to waste a second.

It was equally plain that for a man to be truly free, and therefore free to make the most of his time, he first had to conquer his fear of death. And how best to conquer the fear of death? By believing in something so strongly he is willing to die for it.

From this moment of resolution, Mohandas Gandhi became the most believing, the most *living* man of the twentieth century.

It was on these same lonely marches that he thought his way through to celibacy. He had for some time, off and on since 1900, tried to practice continence. Kasturbai "was never the temptress," he said simply . . . "but it was my weak will and lustful attachment that was the obstacle." Twice he had moved into a separate bedroom. For a while he made it his routine to go to bed only after exhausting himself in heavy physical labor. But desire had always proved stronger than self-control. Now, however, he was determined to take the vow and to live with it. And he did. Though many times "it was like living on the edge of a sword," he was a practicing celibate the last forty-two years of his life.

Why did he do it? While speculative psychiatrists may reasonably offer more complicated motives, Gandhi himself said simply that he had decided that *bramacharya* was indispensable for anyone "aspiring to serve humanity with his whole soul." He would have more and more occasion for service and he would find himself unequal to the task "if I were engaged in the pleasures of family life and in the propagation and rearing of children." During his hours of meditation, in-between campsites, he had come to know the thing "more greatly desired" than those things the *Gita* would have him renounce. That thing was freedom—the freedom to work for the common welfare, to free Indians, to free India, to embrace poverty, to find truth.

He was thirty-seven years old. By the time the Zulu Rebellion was over and he had rejoined Kasturbai in Phoenix, his transformation was complete.

NINE

Satyagraha

He was soon summoned to Johannesburg. The Transvaal legislature, it was reported, was ready to pass a bill that would require every Indian over eight years old to be fingerprinted and registered, presumably as a means of preventing further migration of Indians into the province.

When the full text of the bill was published in the *Transvaal Gazette*, Gandhi was stunned. An Indian could be challenged to produce his registration card at any time, at any place; police officers could enter an Indian's home to examine permits; failure to register was to be punishable by imprisonment, heavy fines, or deportation. Such stringent terms could only mean that the government was determined to drive all Indians out of the Transvaal. If the bill became law, if the Indians submitted to it, it would spell "absolute ruin." It had to be resisted.

Gandhi called a mass meeting for September 11 at the Empire Theater in Johannesburg. Three thousand Indians showed up.

As the main agenda item, he had prepared a resolution condemning the bill as a violation of basic civil rights and announcing the unanimous intent of the Indian community not to comply with its provisions should it pass. It was a strong statement and he was uneasy for fear it might boomerang. Unless the community was prepared to back words with action, it would be worse than no statement at all. And what assurance did he have, really, that these people—most of them poor and easily cowed—would hold fast and move together when the time came for follow-through? Was he guilty of asking more commitment than they were able to give? If so, how else could the authorities read the resolution but as an admission of impotence?

He was sitting on the stage, agonized by doubt, when all of a sudden he was jolted to hear one of the warm-up speakers declare that "in the name of G—" he would never submit to the law. From this impromptu reference to a solemn oath, there now exploded in Gandhi's mind an entire strategy. A feeling surged through him like nothing he had ever experienced before. Where he had been tense and anxious, he was now exhilarated, confident, firmly calm. When he rose to address the crowd, it was as if everything he had been through during the past twelve years, up to and including his recent vow of *bramacharya,* had prepared him for this moment.

"The government," he said, "has taken leave of all sense of decency . . . There is only one course open—to die rather than submit." The struggle would be long, he warned. It meant the risk of imprisonment, starvation, flogging, even death. "But I can boldly declare, and with certainty, that so long as there is even a handful of men true to their pledge there can be only one end to the struggle—and that is victory."

He then called on everyone in the audience to join him in a pledge of resistance till death. He did not specify the form of resistance; he only made it clear that it was to be nonviolent. On cue, his fellow Indians rose, raised their hands, and vowed, "with God as our witness," not to submit to the ordinance if it became law. On that resounding note, the meeting adjourned.

He now had the strategy—nonviolent resistance to an unjust law, carried out by masses sworn to God and psychologically prepared for imprisonment or death. But he had no name for it. He rejected the phrase, "passive resistance." There was to be nothing passive about his movement. More-over, in a meeting with Europeans, he was told that the term was commonly associated with English suffragettes, that it was sometimes characterized by hatred, and that it often manifested itself as violence. At a loss, he offered a nominal prize through *Indian Opinion* to the reader who came up with the best suggestion. The winner was his cousin, Maganlal, who coined a word, *"Sadagraha"—sad* meaning truth and *agraha* meaning firmness or insistence. For the sake of clarity, Gandhi changed it to *Satyagraha*. In Guja-rati *satya* means both truth and love and both are attributes of the soul. *Satyagraha* is thus variously translated as "soul force" or "insistence on truth." Thereafter, Gandhi's organi-zation was known as the *Satyagraha* Association and its mem-bers—the warriors of truth and love—as *Satyagrahis*.

For Gandhi, and in time the entire civilized world, *Satyagraha* was more a process than a strategy. It was not so much a philosophical statement but a slogan—a kind of convenient shorthand for describing either one particular way, or all the various ways, in which he would apply politi-cally the things he kept learning from his "experiments with truth." But at the personal level its emergence in 1906 rep-resented something quite distinct—the final, victorious reso-lution of seemingly irreconcilable emotional conflicts. For with the crystallization of *Satyagraha* he had found a way to see beyond the world of chaos into a universe of order; to stay sane in an insane society; to live inwardly at peace in the midst of pain and injustice; to fight the sickness in man-kind without becoming sickened.

The Black Act, as it was called, was passed, effective July 1, 1907. Indians were given thirty days to register or face the penalties. Gandhi promptly organized for resistance. To provide any waverers with a chance to withdraw, he readministered the oath of resistance to the three thousand who had taken it at the meeting in September, and through the columns of *Indian Opinion* obtained pledges from hundreds more. Through his newspaper he also instituted a practice that was to be an indispensable characteristic of every *Satyagraha* campaign thereafter. He spelled out his plans plainly and unreservedly, not only for the instruction of his co-workers but as a means of serving forthright notice on his opponents.

On the day the registration offices opened, picketing Indians appeared waving posters ("Loyalty to the king demands loyalty to the King of Kings . . . Indians Be Free.") Gandhi placed volunteers outside the permit offices to dissuade the faint of heart, but the volunteers were forbidden to be violent or even discourteous to those who insisted on registering. The first Indian to be arrested became a hero; others immediately clamored to join him in jail. Taken aback, the Transvaal government extended the date of registration.

In late December, Gandhi, with twenty-six of his colleagues, was sentenced to two months simple imprisonment. But where the government's intent was to halt the Indians by locking up their leader, the result was precisely the opposite. Morale remained high, the boycott grew, and before long the Johannesburg jail, built to accommodate fifty, was crowded with a hundred and fifty-five *Satyagrahis*.

Gandhi scarcely had time to adjust to prison routine before he was rushed to Pretoria for a conference with the Governor General, Jan Christian Smuts. Still in prison garb, he stood as Smuts read him the terms of a compromise: The Asiatic Registration Act would be repealed if Indians agreed to register voluntarily. With a smile, Smuts informed Gandhi that he was free and that the other prisoners would be released the next morning.

Within a few hours after his return to Johannesburg, Gandhi called a meeting to explain the agreement he had reached with Smuts. His followers were confused. Some were bitter and all felt let down. Why had he agreed to such a compromise? they demanded to know. Registration, he explained, was aimed at keeping Indians from moving into the Transvaal illegally; since the *Satyagrahis* did not intend to sneak immigrants into the province, why not register?

"To bow to compulsion reduces the individual dignity and stature . . . but collaboration freely given is generous and hence ennobling." But why had he not insisted that the registration act be repealed before, rather than after, voluntary registration? By conceding to Smuts, had he not played into the hands of the government? What if the government broke faith? "A *Satyagrahi*," Gandhi told them, "bids good-bye to fear. . . Even if the opponent plays him false twenty times, the *Satyagrahi* is ready to trust him the twenty-first time, for an implicit trust in human nature is the very essence of his creed."

His manner calmed most of the group except for a six-foot Pathan named Mir Alam. Rising from his seat, he accused Gandhi of having taken a bribe of 15,000 pounds, then, without waiting for a reply, bellowed, "With Allah as my witness, I will kill the man who takes the lead in applying for registration."

Gandhi eyed him gently. The audience quieted to a hush, waiting. "I will be the first to register," Gandhi said and sat down.

On a morning soon thereafter Gandhi walked down Von Brandis Street to the registration office. On his way he

General Jan Christian Smuts, when he was in command of the South African forces during the Boer War.

was accosted by Mir Alam and several of his friends. Apparently with every intent to kill, the giant Pathan struck Gandhi a heavy blow on the head. Gandhi dropped to the sidewalk, unconscious. On his lips were the same words that forty-one years later would be his last: *"He Rama"*—"Oh, God."

Passersby rescued him from further attack. On recovering, his first act was to register, causing thousands of others to follow his example. His second was to obtain the release of Mir Alam and his accomplices, who were being held under arrest. "They thought they were doing right," he told incredulous friends. "I have no desire to prosecute them."

A month went by and it became clear that Smuts was backing out on his part of the compact. Instead of repealing the Black Act, the Transvaal legislature passed a new measure extending its penalties to all future immigrants from India. "Foul Play," called Gandhi in an article in *Indian Opinion*. He wrote Smuts, recalling their conversation. Smuts ignored him.

Had he to do it over again, he would still have trusted Smuts. As a matter of principle, he could not allow himself to predicate any action on distrust. But now the important thing was to make Smuts understand that the Indian community had no intention of acquiescing to a brazenly unjust law. By way of educating Smuts, he staged a huge bonfire in the Hamidia mosque. There 2000 Indians threw their registration certificates into a cauldron of burning paraffin, a demonstration of protest that the *Daily Mail* correspondent compared to the Boston Tea Party. It ended with a telling sign of solidarity when Mir Alam stepped forward to shake Gandhi's hand.

For some time, prominent Indians in Natal who had an old right of domicile in the Transvaal had been pleading with Gandhi to let them test the Transvaal immigration ban. Convinced of their commitment, he now agreed. First he sent one across the border, then another, and then dozens, one of whom was his eldest son, Harilal. Each was arrested and sentenced to three months at hard labor. When Gandhi

Henry David Thoreau, American writer and journalist, whose "Essay on Civil Disobedience" Gandhi read while in jail.

joined them, scores of well-to-do Indian barristers and merchants immediately turned up at police stations stating that they had no registration certificates and demanding that they too be imprisoned, which they were. At one time 2500 Transvaal Indians were in prison. Another 6000 had either been expelled or forced to flee under threat of expulsion. Active defiance continued throughout 1908.

This time Gandhi got a rough taste of prison life. He was worked from seven in the morning till sundown, digging with a spade in the hard ground. Uncomplaining, he cleaned the toilets and, in an effort to improve the prison fare for his seventy-five co-inmates, volunteered to do most of the cooking.

Freed in December, 1908, he was re-arrested for a three-month term beginning in February and transferred to another prison. It was during this sentence that he first read Henry David Thoreau's *Essay on Civil Disobedience* in which the American stated his case for withholding taxes from a government he considered immoral. Much of what

Gandhi read in *Civil Disobedience* so moved him that he copied the lines in his own hand, the better to fix them in his mind. In later years, whenever referring to his many stays in prison, he was given to quoting Thoreau as an apt summary of his own attitude: "I did not feel for a moment confined, and the walls seemed a great waste of stone and mortar."

Out of jail, Gandhi moved to enlist world opinion. Maintaining a steady series of exposés in *Indian Opinion,* he dispatched Henry Polak to India while he himself took off for England. His trip was timely, for plans were under way to merge the four African colonies into the Union of South Africa. London, he was sure, was the best place to lobby for Indian rights.

Viewed long-range, his mission was quite productive. Because of his efforts, British editors and statesmen were once again reminded of the disparities between British ideals and colonial policies. The Indian issue in South Africa, no less than the question of freedom of India itself, was forced to the surface with such skill that from that time forward it could never again be ignored or dismissed by any major political party.

But on his return, he was given several reasons to be disheartened. The British liberals who tried to mediate between the *Satyagraha* Association and the Boers reported a complete breakdown in understanding. On the personal side, he faced a critical decline in income. He had put all his savings in the movement, and since 1906 he had had little time for his law practice. Furthermore, in the absence of visible victories, wealthy Indians had begun to lose interest, and he was hard put to find enough funds to care for the dispossessed families of the imprisoned *Satyagrahis.*

Salvation came in the form of a tall, thick-set square-headed German with a handlebar mustache and pince-nez. His name was Hermann Kallenbach and he described himself variously as architect, Buddhist, pugilist, and wrestler. In Gandhi's words he was a man "of strong feeling, wide sympathies, and childlike simplicity." He had the additional virtue of being wealthy. He had joined the movement the year before and had proved so competent that Gandhi had come to use him as a deputy.

Now, when Gandhi suggested that perhaps the most economical arrangement would be to lodge the dependents of his displaced followers on a communal farm, Kallenbach bought a thousand acres twenty-one miles from Johannesburg and gave them rent free to the movement. They called it Tolstoy Farm after the Russian novelist, Leo Tolstoy, whose essays on Christ's social gospel were an implicit endorsement of nonviolence and renunciation. Depending on the number of *Satyagrahis* in jail, the Farm's population varied between fifty and a hundred.

Gandhi and Kallenbach delightedly joined hands in making the colony a test of all their ideas about diet, child-rearing, physical labor, nonviolence, and education. Their design was that of a cooperative commonwealth and, everything considered, it was incredibly successful, perhaps because of their own contagious, irrepressibly high spirits. The colony had a common vegetarian kitchen (for most of this period Gandhi and Kallenbach lived exclusively on fruits) and everyone, including children, was expected to do his quota of work. Kallenbach was a master of many trades. He taught Gandhi carpentry and shoemaking and supervised a workshop that employed most of the young boys on the farm.

"I prepare the bread," Gandhi wrote a friend. "The general opinion about it is that it is well made . . . I have also learned to prepare caramel coffee."

As general manager, Gandhi was a hard taskmaster, but it was his rule never to ask as much of others as he demanded of himself. When he had case work to do in Johannesburg, he would leave at two in the morning and walk twenty-one miles to his law office at a pace that would get him there before the courts opened. It was not unusual for him to walk as many as fifty miles a day.

He enjoyed most his role as school teacher, although from time to time he was admittedly troubled by the ethical

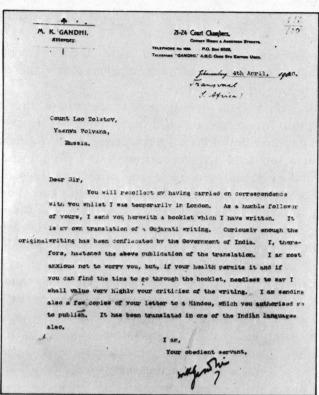

To Leo Tolstoy from Mohandas Gandhi. April 4, 1910.

problems of maintaining discipline. Some of the methods he worked out were instructive, foreshadowing the techniques he later used to tame the British empire. He did not believe in corporal punishment. The best way to inculcate high standards of deportment, he felt, was for the teacher to set a good example. Once, however, he lost his temper with an unruly seventeen-year-old boy and, picking up a ruler, hit him on the arm. The incident shocked Gandhi as much as it did the class and set him searching for "a better method of correcting students." He found it not long thereafter when two of the young residents had what he called a "moral fall." "I felt that the only way the guilty parties could be made to realize my distress and the depth of their own fall would be for me to do some penance." He thereupon imposed upon himself a fast for seven days. As a consequence, "my anger against the guilty parties subsided and gave place to the purest pity for them . . . My penance cleared the atmosphere."

It would be a mistake to assume that the importance of Tolstoy Farm was only as a haven for *Satyagrahis*. As strange as it may have seemed to the Boers of Transvaal, the fact that it existed at all—the fact that a small band of Indians preferred a life of grim austerity, practicing a rare kind of brotherhood—was not without its effect. On General Smuts and others of his persuasion, Tolstoy Farm impressed itself like an animated grievance petition, and to the masses of Indians who were quietly readying themselves for another round of *Satyagraha* its very survival was their inspiration.

In 1912 Gokhale came to South Africa to investigate Indian grievances. Gandhi met him in Capetown and happily served as his secretary, bearer, and valet throughout the one-month tour. After a conference with the ministers of the new Union of South Africa, Gokhale was convinced that everything had been settled. "The Black Act will be repealed," he told Gandhi. General Smuts had even promised to lift the annual tax on serfs who became free laborers.

Gandhi shook his head. "I doubt it very much," he said. "You do not know the ministers as I do."

Gandhi was right. Hardly had Gokhale left the shores of South Africa when General Smuts reneged again. It would not be possible to abolish the three-pound tax on the ex-indentured laborers, Smuts told the South African parliament. European feeling in Natal, he said, was too strongly opposed.

The next year there was an added insult when a justice of the Cape Colony supreme court ruled that only Christian marriages would be recognized as legal. In effect, Hindu, Moslem, and Parsi marriages were invalidated and all Indian wives were declared concubines.

This time it was the women who took the lead.

First, a party of sixteen "sisters" left Phoenix for the Transvaal, eager to confront a government that had so dishonored Indian women. Among them was Kasturbai. "What defect is there in me which disqualifies me for jail?" she demanded when Gandhi tentatively suggested that perhaps she was too weak for the journey.

On September 23, 1913, they were arrested and imprisoned for crossing the border without a permit.

A few days later, Gandhi sent a party of eleven women from Tolstoy Farm into Natal. Obeying his instructions, they proceeded to the Newcastle coal mines where they successfully incited the Indian miners to strike. At this point the women were arrested and the mine owners turned off the lights and water in the company houses. Hurrying to the scene, Gandhi advised the laborers to leave their quarters and pitch camp in the open.

In a few days, about five thousand Indians, all jobless and homeless, were on Gandhi's hands. The *Satyagraha* Association did not have the resources to feed them, nor did the few Christians in the area who had been attracted to their plight. As a way out of the dilemma, Gandhi proposed that the strikers march to the Transvaal and be "safely deposited in jail." He telegraphed his intent to the Natal government, suggesting "the peace army" be arrested before it broke camp. The authorities did not oblige him.

In a little more than a day, on a ration of a pound and a half of bread and an ounce of sugar, the strikers hiked thirty-six miles from Newcastle to Charlestown, close to the Transvaal border. While they paused, Gandhi tried once again to arrange for a peaceful settlement. He telephoned General Smuts's office, telling the General's secretary, "If he promises to abolish the tax, I will stop the march." After checking with Smuts, the secretary replied, "The General will have nothing to do with you."

Gandhi called his forces together and gave them the battle plan. Tomorrow they would cross the border. If, as seemed likely, the Transvaal government refused to arrest them, they would advance to Tolstoy Farm by eight day-marches of twenty miles each. Food would be shipped to every day's campsite. There would be hardships. If any among them were of faint heart, now was the time to reconsider. At the close, he repeated the three standard rules of conduct: *Do not resist arrest; if the police flog you, don't fight back; keep clean.* The next morning, November 6, Gandhi headed a column of 2037 men, 127 women, and 57 children. It was, to quote *The Sunday Post,* "an exceedingly picturesque crew." Most were barefooted. Many of the women carried babies on their backs.

They crossed the border without incident, but they had hardly settled themselves for the night when an officer arrived with a warrant for Gandhi's arrest. At the police station, Gandhi posted bail and rushed back to the camp in time for the next day's march. Twenty miles later, he was re-arrested, this time by a magistrate. Gandhi laughed: "It seems I've been promoted."

Again he was released. But by the fourth day Transvaal authorities were growing uneasy and at Volksrust they ordered him held without bail.

The marchers continued without him as far as Balfour Station. There they were halted, herded into three waiting trains, and shipped back to Natal. But instead of being imprisoned they were forced into wire-enclosed stockades, which the government declared to be "out-stations" of the Dundee and Newcastle jails. And, instead of being put to the usual hard labor, they were sentenced to work at their old jobs in the mines. Workers who refused were whipped. Miners in the north and west who struck in sympathy were chased back to work by mounted military police.

Meanwhile in Volksrust, Gandhi, Polak, and Kallenbach were each sentenced to a year at hard labor. Transferred to Pretoria, Gandhi was put in an unlit cell ten feet long and seven feet wide. He was denied a bench, refused permission to talk, and, when summoned to the court for evidence, handcuffed and manacled like a criminal.

But by now South Africa's "blood-and-iron" policy was too much for a civilized world to contain. Fifty thousand men were on strike, and thousands more in jail. Gokhale toured India, mobilizing moral and financial support. Editorial opinion in both Britain and India was outraged. Breaking the imperial rule of non-interference, the British viceroy in India demanded a commission to inquire into Indian grievances.

Giving in, Smuts released Gandhi and immediately announced the appointment of a commission. Gandhi noted the appointees and promptly branded it a fraud, "a packed body, intended to hoodwink the government and public opinion both of England and of India." (One of its three members had been a leader of the crowd that tried to lynch him on his return to Durban in 1897.) He insisted that one or more Indians, or at least someone known to be pro-Indian, be added.

Sensing victory, but aware that the fight was not yet won, he called a mass meeting that was noteworthy in one particular. He appeared in a knee-length white smock, an elongated loincloth, and sandals. Rarely thereafter was he ever seen in Western clothes.

Smuts would not agree to expand the commission. Seeing no alternative, Gandhi announced a massive protest march from Durban on January 1, 1914. By coincidence, however, the white employees of all South African railways went on strike. With the nation paralyzed, Gandhi's reaction was to cancel the march. It was against the principles of *Satyagraha,* he explained, to take advantage of an opponent's weakness.

In answer to an invitation, Gandhi went to Smuts's office, recalling the broken pledge of 1908 and on his guard against fresh deception. Smuts, it appeared, was as eager as Gandhi to talk terms and to make the terms clear and binding. "This time we want no misunderstanding," Smuts said. "Let all the cards be on the table." Through meetings and correspondence, every clause of the impending agreement was meticulously examined. The resulting document became the Indian Relief Act.

For Gandhi, the crusade was over. The three-pound tax on former indentured Indian laborers was abolished. Non-Christian marriages were legalized; though indentured contract labor would cease in 1920, free Indians could continue to enter the Union, and wives could come from India to join their husbands in South Africa. Though it was admittedly a compromise, Gandhi saw the agreement as a vindication of the principle of racial equality and a clear demonstration of the power of *Satyagraha*.

"Return to India within twelve months," Gokhale had told him on his visit in 1912. Now Gandhi was free to obey. But before he left, he had one thing yet to do. While in jail, he had made a pair of sandals. He sent them as a parting gift to General Smuts.

TEN

Break with the British Empire

He sat on the dais, waiting his turn to speak. He was wearing a *kathiawadi* cloak, a *dhoti,* and a turban, all made of Indian mill-cloth. On the platform with him, some in black cutaways and striped pants, were several important Indian politicians, a maharajah, and a token number of British officials.

It was February, 1916. It had been a year and a half since he left South Africa, a year and one month since he landed in Bombay, a year, almost to the day, since Gokhale's death.

On this day, his thoughts must surely have been of Gokhale, for it was Gokhale who had told him to spend the first year of his return "with his ears open and his mouth shut," refraining from political action. He had spent the year studying and traveling, listening indiscriminately to the grievances of the poor, the platitudes of the bureaucrats, and the brave, bold plans of the young intellectuals. Now his year was up and he was ready to get some things off his mind.

The occasion was the opening of the Hindu University Central College in Benares. The audience included native princes and Indian civil servants, their ambitious sons, and, conspicuously, the splendidly dressed maharajah on whose patronage the college depended. None of them would have

Gandhi in 1916 when he announced that he would foster a Civil Disobedience campaign against British rule in India.

been surprised to hear a bit of anti-British talk, for a certain amount of anti-British talk was fashionable, even in the company of the British. But mostly they expected to be praised and flattered, maybe a little uplifted. The last thing they were prepared to hear was that they should give up their favored positions and go to work in the villages. Which was exactly what Gandhi proceeded to tell them.

He began, in a thin, conversational voice, by making a case for a political philosophy grounded in religion. "Truth is the end; love a means thereto . . . the Golden Rule is to dare to do the right at any cost." He then spoke of the question of independence, his dark brown eyes making polite recognition of the presence of Mrs. Annie Besant, founder of the Home Rule movement. "No amount of speeches will make us fit for self-government," he said emphatically. "It is only our conduct that will fit us for it." He then sounded what was to become the major theme of his life: that the winning of self-government required both (1) a massive

Mrs. Annie Besant—socialist, theosophist, and free thinker. Gandhi first met her in London during his student days. In 1916 she founded the Indian Home Rule League.

commitment to civil disobedience and, at the same time, (2) the organization of India's educated middle class for constructive service among the poor. Foreign rule would be replaced, he said, when Indian leaders began to serve the needs of the villagers better than the British.

His audience was getting edgy. Mrs. Besant, afraid that he would go too far, beseeched him: "Stop it, Mr. Gandhi."

"A superficial study of British history," Gandhi continued, "has made us think that all power percolates to the people from parliaments. The truth is that power resides in the people . . . Our salvation can come only through the farmer. Neither the lawyers nor the doctors nor the rich landlords are going to secure it . . . Whenever I hear of a great palace rising in any great city of India . . . I become jealous at once and I say, 'Oh, it is the money that has come from the farmers.' "

At the prompting of a British officer, the worried chairman interrupted him and tried to shut him up. Gandhi ignored him. Referring to the maharajah whose speech had preceded his, he said, "I feel like saying to these noblemen, 'There is no salvation for India unless you strip yourselves of this jewelry and hold it in trust for your countrymen.' "

The audience gasped. Once again, the chairman told him to sit down.

"If we trust and fear God," Gandhi said, over the nervous coughs and loud whispers of his audience, "we shall have to fear no one, not maharajahs, not viceroys, not the detectives, not even King George."

At that, the audience took up the cry, "Sit down! Sit down!" Hurriedly, the chairman brought the ceremony to a close.

Thus, to the keen discomfort of the educated and the well-to-do, did Gandhi begin his ministry in India.

His year of "probation," as he called it, had in some ways been quite difficult.

At Gokhale's suggestion, Ganadhi, Kasturbai, and Kallenbach had returned to India by way of England. Gokhale was to meet them in London, where he had arranged for a round of interviews with top British statesmen. But two days out from Southampton war was declared and on debarkation Gandhi learned that Gokhale had been stranded in Paris. By the time Gokhale was able to join them, Gandhi had organized Indian residents into an eighty-man ambulance corps for service with the British Army, completed a six-week course in first aid, and come down with pleurisy.

Britain's declaration of war created a new issue for Indian politicians, one on which opinion would become more and more divided as hostilities continued. Those favoring unconditional loyalty to the British were in a distinct minority, mainly the beneficiaries of British patronage. One nationalist faction argued that India should cooperate but only in exchange for specific concessions, up to and including a pledge of dominion status. At the other extreme was an openly seditious group that advocated armed rebellion, on the assumption that Britain did not have the resources both to fight a war in Europe and to suppress insurrection in the colonies. Somewhere in the middle was a group headed by Mrs. Annie Besant, who saw the war largely as a reason for stepping up her ongoing campaign for constitutional reform. What better time to dramatize the lack of democracy in India than when Britain was fighting a war to preserve democracy in Europe?

Gandhi's position confounded all sides. Politicians who knew him as the author of *Hind Swaraj,* a booklet on Indian home rule, were puzzled by his unqualified support of the British. His followers in *Satyagraha* were distressed. Henry Polak cabled from South Africa asking how his organizing an ambulance corps jibed with his advocacy of nonviolence.

To the politicians, Gandhi's answer was that "England's need should not be turned into our opportunity." Besides, there was good reason to believe that after the war Britain would voluntarily grant India self-government. As for his personal participation in the war, he frankly acknowledged its inconsistency with the principles of *ahisma,* nonviolence. "But it is not always given to one to be . . . clear about one's duty. A votary of truth is often obliged to grope in the dark."

He took a long time recovering from pleurisy, perhaps because he insisted on restricting his diet to ground nuts, ripe and unripe bananas, lemons, olive oil, tomatoes, and grapes. (He had refused to drink milk ever since he learned "of the wicked processes" that farmers in Calcutta used to extract the last drop from their cows.) In fact, he was still weak when he left London and was not entirely out of danger until his ship entered the milder climate of Suez.

He landed in Bombay on January 9, 1915, to learn that he had made the government's Honors List for the New Year. There followed several days of banquets and receptions. At one function, staged by Gujaratis in Bombay, the main speaker was Mohammed Ali Jinnah, founder of the Moslem League, who some twenty-five years later would figure as his most committed enemy. Jinnah delivered "a short but sweet" eulogy in English, as did all the other principals. When Gandhi's turn came to express his thanks, he made a point of speaking in his native Gujarati.

From Bombay to Rajkot he traveled third class. When a mystified Brahmn asked him why, he said smiling, "Because there is no fourth class." Before the trip, "the better to pass muster as a poor man," he shed his cloak and turban and bought a cheap Kashmiri cap. So attired—a traditional Hindu *dhoti* around his waist and the cheap cloth cap on his head—he rode or walked through most of India during the next twelve months. Everywhere, he was the subject of lavish attention from Gokhale's political friends and embarrassing adulation from the peasants. At the fair in Hardvar, the "deep impression my humble services in South Africa had made throughout the whole of India" became embarrassingly plain. Pilgrims sought him out in such numbers and with such insistence that he had little time for anything but religious discussion. They would not leave him alone at mealtime, and even followed him into his bath. Already he was hearing cries of "Mahatmaji, Mahatmaji," although it would be a few years before the title, "Great Soul in Peasant's Garb," was fixed on him by India's Nobel Prize-winning poet, Rabindranath Tagore.

In the beginning he had been pleased to take his political cues from Gokhale, feeling "secure in his keeping." Indeed, he had returned "in the ardent hope of merging myself with him," and it was clear that Gokhale, a man who trusted his instincts, saw Gandhi as his successor. He offered to pay all Gandhi's public expenses and when he learned of Gandhi's desire to build an *ashram* in the style of Tolstoy Farm he volunteered to underwrite all the costs.

But Gandhi had been in India hardly a month when Gokhale died suddenly of a stroke. About the same time the necessity to set up the *ashram* became pressing. Eighteen boys from Phoenix, led by Maganlal, had arrived and while a number of friends, including Tagore, were happy to offer them hospitality, Gandhi was anxious to get the family settled.

With the loss of Gokhale's sponsorship, he turned to the wealthy textile manufacturers of Gujarat, the province of his birth. When they obliged with pledges of regular financial support, he chose a pastoral site near the Sabarmati

With the Hindu poet, Rabindranath Tagore, February, 1940. Awarded the Nobel Prize for literature in 1913, Tagore was knighted in 1915. Four years later, however, he gave up his knighthood in protest against British repression. It was he who called Gandhi "Great Soul in Peasant's Garb."

River, four miles north of Gujarat's capital, Ahmedabad. There, with his family and a dozen disciples, he pitched some tents, improvised a kitchen out of canvas and tin, and built the command post for India's spiritual revolution. Occupying a barred room that resembled nothing so much as it did a jail cell, he lived there for the next sixteen years.

After a while the tents were replaced by low, whitewashed huts scattered through a grove of fruit trees. The population grew from twenty-five to two hundred and fifty, including Hindus of all castes and ages and a smattering of Christian scholars from American and European universities. As in Phoenix and on Tolstoy Farm, life was austere, with every occupant expected to perform manual labor on the farm (there was a spinning and weaving department, a cow shed, and a large barn) as well as to teach in one of the neighboring villages. The vows were strict. Every resident was pledged to truth, nonviolence, fearlessness, anti-untouchability, and abstinence from sex, meat, alcohol, and tobacco. There were, of course, no servants. The settlement operated as a familial society and it was early in this period that Gandhi came to be known as Bapu, "father."

He was a loving and, for the most part, a sensible father, who ruled from a base of moral authority. In defiance of Hindu dogma, he once ordered the mercy killing of a calf. *Ahimsa*, he insisted, had to be intelligently interpreted. His admittance of an untouchable family not only created momentary dissension within the *ashram* but so offended his Hindu supporters outside that they stopped sending money. For a while the colony faced seemingly hopeless financial problems, with no reasonable alternative but to move into Ahmedabad's untouchables quarter. Mysteriously, at the crucial moment, a *sheth* drove into the yard, honked his horn, and on Gandhi's appearance thrust into his hands thirteen thousand rupees. It was enough to support the group for a year.

Once during Gandhi's first month in India, an Englishman asked him how long it might be before he would have both the occasion and the resources to launch a *Satyagraha* campaign. Gandhi replied, "Five years or so." It was, as a point of fact, only four years before the first mass protest and even less before he had an opportunity to put on a one-man demonstration of civil disobedience.

Early in 1917, answering an insistent plea from a peasant, he went to Champaran to investigate alleged conditions among the sharecroppers. Champaran lies in the foothills of the Himalayas, near the remote kingdom of Nepal in the state of Bihar, sometimes known as Buddha's land of monasteries. There, for more than half a century, a million Indian peasants had cultivated land rented from Englishmen. Under a legally enforced system known as *tinkathia*, they were required to plant fifteen per cent of their fields with indigo and to turn over the harvest to the owners as rent; on the rest of the land they could grow anything they chose. If for any reason the farmers stopped growing indigo, the contracts authorized the landlords to raise the rent.

Shortly after 1900, some ingenious Germans developed a synthetic that caused a collapse in the world market for natural indigo. Thereupon the English landlords ordered the sharecroppers to stop planting indigo and subsequently sent them notices of rent increases. When the farmers refused to pay the increases, the landlords coerced them by confiscating their crops, sacking their homes, and impounding their cattle. If they persisted in non-compliance, they were beaten.

When Gandhi came on the scene, the trouble had been going on for five years.

His first move was to get the facts. But when he sought information from the British Landlords' Association he was told by the secretary that the Association did not talk to "outsiders." When he called on the British Commissioner, he was insulted and told to leave. He had no choice, therefore, but to build his case by touring the countryside and interviewing the tenants.

One day, on his way to check reports that a farmer had been flogged, he was riding to a village on an elephant when he was overtaken by a policeman. Driven back to town, he was charged with threatening the public peace and ordered to quit the district "by the next available train." When he refused, he was ordered to stand trial the next day. Overnight, word spread to the peasants of Champaran that the *"maharajah"* who had come to save them had been arrested. By daylight, thousands were standing in attitudes of brooding rebellion all around the courthouse. Alarmed, the police asked Gandhi to help regulate the crowd, which he obligingly did. He did not, however, agree to a postponement of the case, as the government pleader most earnestly suggested. Instead, he read a brief prepared statement:

"As a law-abiding citizen, my first instinct would be . . . to obey the order served upon me. But I could not do so without doing violence to my sense of duty to those whom I came to serve . . . Amid this conflict of duties, I could only throw the responsibility of removing me . . . on the administration . . . It is my firm belief that under the complex constitution under which we are living, the only safe and honorable course for a self-respecting man is, in the circumstances such as face me, to do what I have decided to do—that is, submit without protest to the penalty of disobedience."

The nervous magistrate, uncertain of the constitutional angles, decided to delay pronouncing sentence and ordered Gandhi to be released on bail. When Gandhi refused to furnish bail, the magistrate ordered him released anyway. Several days later, apparently on orders from the lieutenant governor, the case was dropped.

It was a triumph of no little significance. Not only had the cowed and despairing peasants been shown how to use a new weapon against the authorities, they had been given a new model for courage and dignity. "What I did was a very simple thing," Gandhi told them. "I declared that the British could not order me around in my own country."

For the next seven months, he and his co-workers meticulously collected statements from 20,000 tenants. Wherever he went he found time to tend the sick. In one village he set up a small clinic, persuading an Indian social service organization to subsidize the cost of a doctor for six months. He opened primary schools in six villages with volunteer teachers from the *ashram*. Observing him at work, a young British officer wrote his superior: "We may look on Mr. Gandhi as an idealist, a fanatic, or a revolutionary . . . But to the *ryots* he is their liberator, and they credit him with extraordinary powers. He moves about in the villages, asking them to lay their grievances before him, and he is transfiguring the imaginations of masses of ignorant men with visions of an early millennium."

As the work progressed, the government became concerned over the possible implications of Gandhi's findings. The upshot was that the governor of Bihar appointed a commission of inquiry, the Champaran Agrarian Committee. Surprisingly, the Committee endorsed Gandhi's report and not long thereafter an agrarian reform law was passed. Under its provisions the landlords were prohibited from raising rents any further and required to refund twenty-five per cent of the increase already collected.

Meanwhile, at Ahmedabad, a festering dispute between textile mill workers and their employers had reached the stage of crisis. With the outbreak of plague in August, 1917, the mill owners had begun paying bonuses, sometimes amounting to as much as eighty per cent of wages, in an effort to keep the workers from deserting their jobs and fleeing to places where the disease hadn't hit. But now that the epidemic was over, the owners wanted to revert to the old wage scale. The workers thought this grievously unfair in view of the fact that living costs had more than doubled as a result of the war.

At the urging of the British Collector, Gandhi agreed to seek a compromise and for a while it looked as if the disagreement might be quickly resolved. He persuaded both parties to submit to arbitration. But before the arbiters could go to work, a bunch of hotheads at one of the mills walked off their jobs, an action that the mill owners took as a breach of faith. The owners then withdrew from the arbitration agreement and threatened "united action" against all hands, issuing an order to the effect that any worker would be fired who turned down a bonus of twenty per cent.

The strike that ensued became, under Gandhi's command, an almost perfectly ritualized example of his nonviolent technique.

First, he insisted that the millhands ask for no more than what was considered fair and right. (What they had been demanding, he said, was plainly out of the question.) They should, however, be prepared to die rather than take less. After some thought, he decided that they were entitled to a thirty-five per cent increase and got them to go along.

Next, at a mass meeting, he lined out the basic rules of conduct:

(1) The workers must never resort to violence. ("Do nothing and say nothing," he told them, "that will damage the good names of your opponents.")

(2) They must never molest the blacklegs, as the company men were called.

(3) They must not depend on alms. (They were to use their free time constructively, either in other gainful employment or in performing constructive community services.)

(4) They must remain firm no matter how long the strike continued.

In every subsequent meeting, some of which were attended by as many as a thousand workers, Gandhi had the men repeat these rules in the form of a pledge. *Ek Tek*—"Keep the Pledge"—became the strike motto.

As chief negotiator, he maintained a mood of ingratiating gaiety. He took the initiative in arranging talks with the mill owners, most of whom were his personal friends. He told them precisely what the grievances were and what he intended to do. At the outset, he made it clear that his intent was not to cast blame or to vilify the mill owners but to persuade management and workers to come to the kinds of terms that would permit an equal measure of self-esteem. He was careful to give the mill owners every opportunity to change their minds with grace. At his invitation, he and the chief management negotiator had lunch on the *ashram* grounds practically every day.

But it was not easy to sustain morale among the workers, and after the first week their spirits began to sag. Without work, few of them had the means to exist, and, since Gandhi had forbidden them to beg, it began to look as if they would have no choice but to give in. Some, breaking their pledges, began menacing the blacklegs. Others joined the scabs in the mills.

At a mass meeting on the seventeenth day, Gandhi was told of new defections. Distressed, he made up his mind. "Unless the strikers rally," he told the group, "and continue the strike until a settlement is reached . . . I will not touch any food." The workers were shocked. "Not you but we should fast," they said. He shook his head. Had he not declared at the beginning of the strike that if it led to starvation he would be the first to starve? "There's no need for you to fast," he told them. "It would be enough if you could remain true to your pledge."

Thus he declared his first public fast. Though its announced aim was to rally the workers, it proved equally effective in putting pressure on the mill owners. On the third day, the owners agreed to submit to impartial arbitration and shortly thereafter decided jointly to give the workers a thirty-five per cent bonus. The twenty-one-day strike ended in an atmosphere of "good cheer and accord," with a distribution of sweets all round.

All during World War I Gandhi remained true to his vow to do nothing that would embarrass the British government. His political activities were confined to small localities and carefully controlled to prevent their being inflated into national issues. He was critical of the more militant Indian nationalists; to his ear, they sounded as jingoistic as the British colonials. He behaved as if it were ordained that Britain would grant self-government after the war, buoyed in his belief by the readiness with which opinion in the

Western world had received Woodrow Wilson's doctrine of self-determination. He declined Mrs. Annie Besant's invitation to help found the Home Rule League, telling his friends, "I could only join an organization to affect its policy."

Fundamentally, his attitude toward Britain was inseparable from his attitude toward India. "When Indians qualify for freedom," he said, "England will grant them freedom." To qualify, in his terms, meant that Indians would have to demonstrate an ability to organize, to show that they had both the will and the discipline to run their own affairs. Perhaps most of all, they would have to forget their religious differences. He grieved for India as it was, agreeing with Tagore, who saw it as "the eternal ragpicker at other people's dust bins." Also like Tagore, he felt that India's condition

American President
Woodrow Wilson enunciated his famous doctrine of self-determination during World War I. It led Gandhi to believe that Britain would grant self-rule to India when the war was over.

was self-made and self-perpetuating. (In one of his most famous poems, Tagore wrote: "Prisoner, tell me who was it that wrought this unbreakable chain? 'It was I,' said the prisoner, 'who forged this chain very carefully.'") Gandhi always put content before form. He wanted freedom for India but, more, he wanted a new and free Indian individual. He confounded many self-styled patriots by insisting that the methods of the ruler were more important than his nationality. He set himself particularly at odds with those who argued that the British should be driven out by force, and that, once free, India should develop its own army and empire. "You would have English rule without the Englishman," he said . . . "the tiger's nature without the tiger. You would make India English . . . This is not the *swaraj* that I want."

For a time, he had reasons to be encouraged. Coincidental with the December 1916 meeting at Lucknow of the predominantly Hindu Indian National Congress, a pact was signed with the Moslem League pledging joint participation "in any patriotic efforts for the advancement of the country as a whole." Less than a year later, the Secretary of State for India, Sir Edward S. Montague, announced a new British policy that promised the establishment of "self-governing institutions with a view to the progressive realization of responsible government in India." Like most of his colleagues, Gandhi interpreted Montague's statement as a pledge of dominion status.

In 1918, when the war was going badly for the Allies, Gandhi exhausted himself in a largely unsuccessful effort to recruit Indian troops for the British army. He went into virtually every village in Gujarat, traveling sometimes in a bullock cart but more often by foot.

The heat, the dust, and the unaccustomed food proved too much for him. He was struck low by a serious attack of dysentery. Brought back to Ahmedabad, he was taken to a mill owner's magnificent home for treatment, but he refused the attentions of a doctor and his own dietary cures did no good at all. When his health continued to fail, he insisted on being transferred to the *ashram*. Weak and emaciated, he resigned himself to death. "My last message to India," he told the *ashram's* residents as part of his good-bye ceremony, "is that she will find her salvation through nonviolence; and through nonviolence alone India will contribute to the salvation of the world." Of his life, he said sadly: "I have taken up things only to leave them half done." He was forty-nine.

That he did not die was due partly to the arrival of a doctor of dubious credentials who gave him ice therapy. But a more important factor was undoubtedly Kasturbai, who at the crucial moment persuaded him to drink goat's milk on the grounds that his vow of abstinence applied only to cow's milk. In his autobiography, he confessed to having compromised: "My will to live proved stronger than my devotion to truth."

A half million Indians fought on the side of the British during World War I. Britain, however, did not make the mistake of equating military service with loyalty to the empire. On the contrary, the government of India viewed the progress of the home-rule movement with mounting apprehension. Bal Gangadhar Tilak, the leading nationalist, and Mrs. Annie Besant were flagrantly anti-British. Convinced that if they were not stopped they would soon incite the country to revolution, the government imprisoned them both, along with the two most powerful Moslem leaders, the brothers Shakut and Mohammed Ali. Shortly thereafter, following trials before secret tribunals, thousands of their followers were likewise jailed. Widespread censorship was invoked, and among the books banned was Gandhi's *Hind Swaraj*.

Gandhi's disillusionment began shortly after the armistice in November. Instead of repealing the wartime restrictions, Britain sent a commission headed by Sir Sidney Rowlatt to assess the evidence of sedition in India. Finding plenty, the commission recommended that the laws suppressing free speech, free press, and right of assembly be kept and extended.

When legislation was introduced to carry out Rowlatt's recommendations, Gandhi was outraged. Though still weak from dysentery, he issued a statement branding the measure "unjust, subversive of the principle of liberty, and destructive of the elementary rights of the individual." In February, 1919, he circulated a petition that was frankly subversive: "In the event of these bills becoming law, and until they are withdrawn, we shall refuse civilly to obey. In this struggle we shall faithfully follow truth and refrain from violence to life, person, and property." To recruit signatories, he organized the *Satyagraha Sabha* (rough translation: The Truth-In-Action Society) and began a tour of the country.

On March 18, the New Delhi Imperial Legislative Council passed the Rowlatt Acts. The next morning, in Madras, Gandhi woke up and informed his host that an idea had come to him in a dream. "We should call on the country to observe a general *hartal*."

He moved immediately from dream to action. A *hartal*—that is, a strike—is not an uncommon method in India of mourning or registering protest. But what Gandhi proposed was something different—a one-day national strike combined with a religious sacrament. On a scale heretofore unknown, it was to be a day on which no business was to be conducted and every Indian, regardless of faith or sect, would be expected to fast and pray. Seasoned Congress leaders were inclined to scoff, especially at the religious emphasis. "I am not ashamed to repeat before you," he told them, "that this is a religious battle . . . an attempt to revolutionize the political outlook. I believe that it is possible to introduce uncompromising truth into the political life of the country." When they pointed out that only six hundred men and women had signed the pledge in Bombay, he reminded them that he had won with even fewer *Satyagrahis* in South Africa.

The *hartal* was called for April 6 and the response exceeded Gandhi's most optimistic hopes. Almost the whole of India closed down. Business and government, even in the smallest villages, were paralyzed for twenty-four hours. In the big cities millions marched in seemingly endless parades. One of the most encouraging things to Gandhi, and conversely one of the most disheartening to the government, was what a British publication acknowledged to be "the unprecedent fraternization between the Hindus and the Moslems."

But the *hartal* was hardly the peaceful demonstration that Gandhi had planned. In Delhi, Bombay, Ahmedabad, and other large cities, there were distressing incidents of violence. Telegraph wires were cut, trains blocked, stores looted, Englishmen assaulted. Dismayed, Gandhi fasted for three days and asked his followers to fast for twenty-four hours. But then news came of more violence, this time in small towns in remote provinces. So, twelve days after the *hartal,* he called off the entire *Satyagraha* campaign. Plainly, he had launched civil disobedience before the people were ready. Through a "Himalayan miscalculation," he had grievously underestimated the latent forces of violence.

Indian Lancers, who fought with distinction for the British Empire in World War I, file along a road in Flanders, Belgium, near the front lines.

In the Sikh province of Punjab, post-*hartal* rioting reached tragic proportions. In Amritsar, a city of 150,000, the *hartal* itself had passed without incident. But three days later the government expelled two local leaders of the Congress party. In retaliation, a mob swept through the streets, burning the town hall and post office and killing three prominent Englishmen.

The Punjab government decided that the time had come to get tough. To Amritsar now came Brigadier General Reginald E.H. Dyer of the regular British army, an old Indian hand who as a matter of policy dealt with "the natives" as if at any moment the mutiny of 1857 were likely to recur. On April 12, he issued a proclamation forbidding processions and meetings. On April 13, the day of the Baisakhi Festival, occurred the Amritsar Massacre.

According to an official report, that afternoon General Dyer was told of plans for a mass meeting about 4:40. The meeting was held in Jallianwalla Bagh, a rectangular garden enclosed by walls on three sides. Somewhere between ten and twenty thousand people attended and when General Dyer appeared with his troops they were listening to an address by a man on a raised platform, about 150 yards from the one narrow access.

As the general later explained, his troops were armed "only" with rifles, the entrance being too narrow for the armored cars that carried his machine guns. Without warning, he gave the order to fire, causing the panic-stricken Indians to rush to the side of the compound with the lowest wall, which was five feet high. As they scrambled hysterically for an escape, Dyer's troops fired 1650 rounds in ten minutes. To the official commission of inquiry, Dyer admitted that he would have fired longer had his ammunition held out.

Estimates of the number killed varied from 379 to 400. The number of wounded was reported in excess of 1200. The dying were left all night without water or medical attention. In a dispatch to his superiors, General Dyer wrote, "It was no longer a question of merely dispersing the crowd, but of producing a sufficient moral effect, not only on those who were present but more especially throughout the Punjab." He subsequently made two statements which forever afterward made him the symbol of all that was worst about British rule. "I think it was quite possible I could have dispersed the crowd without firing," he said, "but they would have come back again and laughed, and I should have made what I considered a fool of myself . . . I thought I would be doing a jolly lot of good."

Martial law prevailed throughout the Punjab for the next two months. On orders from General Dyer, Indians were forced to crawl on their bellies in the street where a European woman had been assaulted. Indian-owned automobiles were confiscated. Troops were ordered to disperse crowds wherever they were assembled, regardless of their purpose. The orders were so rigidly interpreted that on several occasions village funeral parades were machine-gunned from the air.

Events in the Punjab marked the beginning of Gandhi's break with the British empire. In November he was invited to attend a Moslem-Hindu conference to consider unified action if Britain ignored Moslem sentiment in the drafting of peace terms with Turkey. On one of the few occasions in his life when he acted without first getting the facts, Gandhi was persuaded to the Moslem view that the caliphate should be preserved. The caliphate was the spiritual dominion of Islam, ruled historically by a caliph who was also the sultan of Turkey. Now it began to appear that the British were going to depose the sultan-caliph, in violation of what Moslems in India had taken to be an ironclad promise of leniency. They were furious.

It was at this conference, hitchhiking on an idea presented by an earlier speaker, that Gandhi first proposed massive non-cooperation as a means of protest. "It is an inalienable right of the people . . . to withhold cooperation," he told the Moslem leaders. He said they should not be satisfied with boycotting British cloth as had been proposed; effective resistance could be achieved only if everything British—

King George V, shown here in full dress naval uniform, announced the Indian Reform Act in 1919.

schools, honors, courts, jobs—were rejected. The Moslems were more alarmed than intrigued by his suggestion and politely tabled it.

Within a month, the government had turned conciliatory. The Indian National Congress was permitted to hold its 1919 annual meeting near Amritsar. Most of the political prisoners, including the two Ali brothers, were released in time to attend. Almost concurrently, King George V announced the Indian Reforms Act, promising amnesty and the prospect that some provincial ministries would be handed over to Indians. Though he did not consider the reforms "wholly satisfactory," Gandhi did believe that the Congress should accept them, and drafted a resolution to that effect. Despite strong opposition, his resolution passed.

Gandhi, however, had expressed a reservation: "It remains to be seen whether it (the Act) will filter down to the Civil Service." That March, twenty martial-law prisoners from the Punjab were sentenced to death. It was a judgment that Gandhi viewed as a clear violation of the announced amnesty. As if to add insult to injury, the viceroy exonerated General Dyer. The official report of the inquiry commission deplored the massacre but made no recommendations, either for recompense or retribution.

In June, incensed Moslems meeting in Allahabad announced that they were ready for Gandhi's campaign of non-cooperation, and authorized him to launch it thirty days after serving notice on the viceroy. In September, the campaign was similarly adopted at a special session of the Indian National Congress. For the next several months, preaching resistance through unity, Gandhi toured the country with the Ali brothers. He was exhilarated. Religious differences, which so often before had cast Hindus and Moslems into warring camps, seemed to be forgotten. Moslems listened to him as attentively as Hindus. At meetings of Moslem women he was the only male considered pure enough to be present without bandaging his eyes.

When the Congress met for its regular session in December, Gandhi had reached the point of no return. Now the unchallenged leader of the party, he offered the resolution that proclaimed independence as the only acceptable goal.

The 1920 Congress, attended by no less than 14,582 official delegates, was both a watershed in British-Indian relations and a landmark in the development of a uniquely Indian political system.

Approving Gandhi's draft of a revised constitution, the party for the first time formally embraced the principles of *Satyagraha,* defining as its creed the attainment of *swaraj* (freedom) "by all legitimate and peaceful means." The small towns and villages were allowed representation and machinery was set up for conducting business between the annual conventions. The effect was to change the Congress from a once-a-year forum dominated by the upper and middle classes into a lively, year-round political organization in touch with the masses.

On Gandhi's motion, the full Congress endorsed the program of non-cooperation. It voted against further collaboration with the British, called for the wearing of homespun clothing exclusively, and condemned the laws of untouchability. But the support of non-cooperation was by no means unanimous. It passed, in fact, thanks largely to the enthusiasm of the rank-and-file delegates of the lower middle class with whom Gandhi had come so thoroughly to identify. He was opposed by all the famous old Congress leaders except Motilal Nehru. His program was obviously a threat to the propertied classes, for it would have them boycott the imperial office, abandon their legal practices, work among the poor in the villages, and ultimately go to jail. The patrician and finicky Mohammed Ali Jinnah, who

Motilal Nehru, father of Jawaharlal, had been close to the British in India but was converted to the cause of India's independence. He became one of Gandhi's most enthusiastic followers in the Civil Disobedience movement.

until then had been a vocal champion of Hindu-Moslem unity, cried out against Gandhi's doctrine. When he was overridden, he walked out of the meeting and out of the party.

Gandhi, however, was resolute. He told delegates that if India's non-cooperation remained nonviolent, self-government would arrive in a year. When the meeting was over, he sent his two South African medals to the viceroy, saying: "I can retain neither respect nor affection for a government which has been moving from wrong to wrong in order to defend its immorality."

By Gandhi's preferred timetable, *Satyagraha* in 1920 may have been premature. He admitted to the grave risks in non-cooperation. Its success presumed an unprecedented degree of self-control on the part of the masses. But to him the risks for India were far greater if *Satyagraha* was not used. Collective anger against the British was now at an alarming high. The Moslems were at the point of rebellion, for England had fulfilled their worst fears by imposing what they considered to be excessively harsh peace terms on Turkey. Freedom-minded young people were agitating for full-scale revolt, arguing that now was the most propitious time, while England was involved in post-war crises on a half-dozen fronts.

So, ready or not, Gandhi saw *Satyagraha* as the only reasonable alternative to pending violence. His decision was that of a masterful politician. He had embraced a recognizable popular goal, home rule, for not to have done so would have been to default his leadership. At the same time, through the force of his own personality, he had been able to adapt the popular goal to his own means and methods. At fifty, he had acquired a degree of power granted few other men in the history of the world.

He was now irrevocably the Mahatma, seen by millions as a reincarnation of God, a saintly figure God-lent for their liberation. On his tours of the countryside, they came by the hundreds of thousands—not so much to hear him, for

127

these were the days before public-address systems and Gandhi's voice was hardly audible, but to see him, to be near him, to touch him, merely to be in his presence. At night his feet and shins would often be covered with scratches made by men, women, and children who had thrown themselves in his path. In one village, people wired that if his train did not stop at their station they would lie down on the tracks and be run over. The train reached the village in the middle of the night. The crowd was waiting. When Gandhi appeared, sleepy-eyed, the people sank to their knees in a single motion and wept.

These were people who would do his bidding without asking, who would follow without understanding. Though he felt a responsibility toward them that was awesome, their unthinking adoration sometimes revolted him. When the Gond tribe began worshipping him, he cried out in horror. "I have expressed my strongest disapproval of this type of idolatry," he said. He wanted Indians to follow in his steps, not kiss his feet.

The non-cooperation movement was meticulously planned. Sensitive to charges that he was opening the gates to anarchy, he created a Congress-sponsored counterpart for every British institution being abandoned by his followers. Parents and teachers who walked out of schools run by the governments were to organize new "national" schools and colleges; lawyers and their clients who boycotted the British courts were to argue their cases before arbitration boards; Indians resigning from the police force and army were expected to become Congress volunteers in the villages. Of most importance was what he conceived as the positive side of *swadeshi*, *swadeshi* being the boycott of British-made cloth. He called not merely for a boycott but for a revival of India's oldest cottage industry, hand-spinning.

To those peasants unable to make an adequate living off the land, and that now included most of them, the spinning wheel offered a chance to supplement incomes in normal years and the means of subsistence during the years of famine and flood. He himself took to spinning half an hour a day, calling it "a sacrament" that turned his mind Godward. *Khadi*—homespun or home-woven cloth—became the party's uniform. By September, 1921, he had adopted the peasant's loincloth as his only costume.

The campaign was planned to develop in phases, beginning with a surrender of titles and honorary offices and ending with mass civil disobedience and non-payment of taxes. He would call for mass disobedience only after the Congress had proved its strength by enlisting ten million members, raising three million dollars for constructive service institutions, and selling two million spinning wheels.

The great Tagore led the way by giving up his knighthood. The wealthiest Indian attorneys—among them the two Nehrus, Motilal and his thirty-one-year-old son, Jawaharlal—quit the British courts forever. Under Gandhi's direction, a small army of peaceful volunteers fanned out into the villages, preaching non-cooperation, teaching literacy and sanitation. Wherever they could, they sold spinning wheels, and where they could not, they gave them away. Throughout the hottest months of 1921, traveling usually in crowded, dirty trains, accompanied sometimes by the Moslem Ali brothers, Gandhi undertook a campaign of political evangelism. A natural dramatist, he climaxed most of his talks by inviting his audience to strip themselves of all foreign clothing. After they had piled it before him—in heaps that the British could quickly translate into the dollars and cents of lost revenue—he would strike a match and, as the clothing burned, tell his audience to go home and start spinning their way to *swaraj*. "In burning my foreign clothing," he would say, "I burn my shame." Crowds as large as a hundred thousand attended some of these demonstrations and their fervor made a few of Gandhi's closest friends uneasy. Tagore warned the Mahatma that the fires that consumed foreign clothing could also inflame men's minds.

In the beginning, the government of India took an official position of "non-interference." In the words of Lord Chelmsford, it dismissed non-cooperation as "the most foolish of all foolish schemes." But before the year was out, the government felt compelled to take stringent action. When the Prince of Wales visited Bombay in November, Gandhi's followers turned on Europeans and Parsis who refused to join them in a boycott of the official ceremonies. In the ensuing riot, fifty-eight persons were killed and three hundred and eighty-one injured. The British reacted by arresting nearly thirty thousand people, outlawing meetings and processions, and raiding Congress and Moslem offices.

When in December the Congress met in Ahmedabad for its annual meeting, the country was seething and Gandhi was faced with another test of leadership. To the Congress membership, he could report progress, but not enough. The fund for constructive service had been oversubscribed and the two million spinning wheels had been distributed, but

Edward, Prince of Wales, poses with British and Indian dignitaries during his visit to India in 1921. Gandhi and his followers boycotted the welcoming ceremonies for the future King Edward VIII.

the party roster still numbered fewer than the announced goal of ten million. Perhaps most important for its effect on his following, a year was up and the self-government that he had predicted was far from being realized.

The work of the past twelve months had awakened the Indian masses to a sense of their own power, but, clearly, the masses were yet to learn how to use that power responsibly. The critical question was whether in a pinch Gandhi could control the masses. He had quieted the Bombay rioters by going on a five-day fast but this, after all, was influence after the fact. Immediately before and during the riots, his non-cooperators had broken ranks so readily that he had to fight the feeling of personal betrayal. "The *swaraj* that I have witnessed during the last two days has stunk in my nostrils," he said in a message to the people of Bombay. "With nonviolence on our lips we have terrorized those who have differed from us."

He came now to Ahmedabad, the memory of Bombay fresh in his mind, to face angry demands from the party's young radicals for an armed rebellion against the British. Two thousand party members were already in jail. Was the party response to be only submission? the young rebels wanted to know. Was Gandhi going to stand by, doing nothing, until all opportunity for protest had been lost? Obviously, they argued, the British were planning further repressive measures, and it was equally obvious that force was the only language the British understood. But Gandhi stood firm, drawing from his spiritual reservoir an appeal that the dissenters could not match. "If India takes up the doctrine of the sword," he told the Congress, "she may gain momentary victory, but then India will cease to be the pride of my heart." Unwilling to defy him, the young then pressed him to launch *Satyagraha's* ultimate weapon—mass civil disobedience. Gandhi agreed, but only if he could test it first in some small area where he could control it. Before adjournment, he was elected the Congress' sole executive officer. The members pledged to act only at his direction.

Gandhi made one last public appeal to Great Britain. The

government's answer was to imprison ten thousand more Congress party members.

With his customary care, Gandhi laid his plans. His intent was to launch civil disobedience in one district; if it succeeded there he would extend it into the adjacent district and from there to the next adjacent district, until the entire country had been freed. For the test, he chose Bardoli, a district of 87,000 people near Bombay in his native Gujarat. He made sure that the people there understood the risks. For refusing to pay taxes they could expect to have their crops auctioned, their lands confiscated, their cattle driven away. To his followers elsewhere he gave clear warning: if violence broke out in any form, the movement would lose its character, "even as a lute would begin to emit notes of discord the moment a single string snaps."

Impatient party leaders in Guntur, a southern district of about a hundred villages, did not wait for the Bardoli test and launched non-payment of taxes without Gandhi's authorization. Taken aback, Gandhi gave them his blessing nevertheless, together with a stern warning to stick to nonviolence. When, despite several threats of reprisal, ninety-five per cent of the Guntur peasants withheld their taxes, all India stirred with a new, exhilarating consciousness of pride, power, and promise.

On February 1, 1922, Gandhi sent his usual open letter to the enemy—in this case, Lord Reading, the new viceroy —outlining meticulously the steps he intended to take. But hardly had the viceroy replied and hardly the campaign in Bardoli begun, when news came of an atrocity. A crazed Indian mob had run wild in the small town of Chauri Chaura eight hundred miles away. Enraged when local constables interfered with a legally authorized procession, the villagers had forced twenty-one policemen and a sub-inspector to flee to the city hall for safety. The villagers had then set fire to the building. According to one report, "the self-imprisoned constables had to come out for dear life and as they did so they were hacked to pieces. Their mangled remains were thrown into the raging flames." Appalled,

Gandhi concluded once again that he had miscalculated. He promptly called off the Bardoli experiment, suspended all plans for a mass campaign, and forbade any acts in defiance of the British government.

His sudden action dismayed his colleagues. From jail Motilal Nehru and Rajpat Rai, who saw Chauri Chaura as only an isolated incident, urged him to reconsider. C. R. Das was described by a fellow prisoner as "beside himself with anger and sorrow at the way Mahatma Gandhi was repeatedly bungling." Young Jawaharlal Nehru was bitter. "Why?" he demanded. "Why pull back when we seem to be consolidating our position on all our fronts?" To which Gandhi replied: "It is a million times better to *appear* untrue before the world than to *be* untrue to ourselves."

Lord Reading was Viceroy of India from 1921 to 1926. In 1922, Gandhi sent him an open letter declaring the steps he was planning to take in opposition to the government.

133

Almost simultaneously, the British government set free its fifty thousand political prisoners and arrested Gandhi for sedition. The viceroy's intent, obviously, was to humiliate Gandhi in the eyes of his followers, choosing a time when his popularity was at an all-time low. But the authorities made a mistake, which they were careful never to repeat during the remaining twenty-five years they had to deal with Gandhi. They tried him in open court.

The trial opened on March 18 in the crowded little courtroom in Ahmedabad. When Gandhi arrived, dressed in a loincloth, the entire court rose in homage. He pleaded his own case. "I am here," he said, ". . . to invite, and cheerfully submit to, the highest penalty that can be inflicted upon me for what in law is a deliberate crime and what appears to me to be the highest duty of a citizen." He then described how his attitude toward Great Britain had changed from that of a "staunch loyalist" to an uncompromising "disaffectionist and non-cooperator." He had come reluctantly to the conclusion that "the British connection" had made India more helpless than she ever was before, politically and economically. Britain, he said, had constructed "a subtle but effective system of terrorism" that had effectively "emasculated the people." Under the circumstances, he considered it "an honor to be disaffected" and asked for the "severest penalty." Before he sat down, he had become the prosecutor and the British Empire the defender.

There was a long pause. Mr. Justice Broomfield bowed and said, "Even those who differ from you in politics look upon you as a man of high ideals and of noble, even saintly life."

He then sentenced Gandhi to six years.

ELEVEN

The Salt March

The British meant to put him out of sight and out of mind. He was kept strictly separated from other political prisoners. For the first several months he was allowed neither a pillow nor a spinning wheel. The authorities would not trust him with a pocket knife to slice his bread and it was only upon intervention of higher authorities that he was allowed a few books on religion and a dictionary. Curiously, in deference to his status, the jailers gave him an African prisoner as an "attendant." Since Gandhi had nothing to be attended to and undoubtedly would not have allowed anybody to attend to it if he had, the action is noted in history as one of many small evidences of bureaucracy's very large inability to understand an individual.

It took some time for Gandhi to learn how to communicate with his cellmate. They spoke different languages and although Gandhi was adept at signs, his overtures to the Negro had to pass through a wall of fear and submissiveness. One day, however, the African was bitten by a scorpion. Gandhi sucked out the poison and treated the wound until it was healed. Thereafter the African was his brother.

In time, the authorities relaxed their restrictions, and for two years Gandhi spent his days writing his autobiography, spinning, and reading. He began and closed each day with prayers. By his own count, he read 150 books, among them Rudyard Kipling's *Barrack Room Ballads*.

In January, 1924, Gandhi suffered an attack of acute appendicitis. Fearing that if he died in their hands India would riot, the British hastily summoned Hindu surgeons. When it appeared that their prisoner was too ill to wait, they obtained his permission for a British doctor to operate. On February 5, still apprehensive, they let him go, pleased and relieved to have him convalesce in freedom.

In releasing Gandhi prematurely, the British took few risks. "The structure so painfully erected by Mr. Gandhi has crumbled hopelessly," read the Government's report to the King. During his absence a serious split had developed between Congress leaders, mostly over the issue of non-cooperation with the government's so-called "Reformed Constitution." Whereas Gandhi had argued for a complete boycott of the new legislative councils, a strong faction, headed by Motilal Nehru and C. W. Das, had sought and won seats in the central legislative assembly.

Worse, his two years in jail had been marked by a series of riots of increasing ferocity between Hindus and Moslems. Hindu politicians had become alarmed by the spirit of communalism among Moslems that had resulted from a melding of the caliphate movement with Gandhi's non-cooperative campaign. By the same token, Moslem leaders had come to reconsider the implications of a cooperative effort with Hindus that had as its goal an all-Indian community in which they would inevitably be outnumbered. At the neighborhood level, the tension expressed itself in a recurrent exchange of insults to each other's rituals and in vituperative quarrels over the distribution of state patronage. Whereas only two years before, in the interest of amity, Moslems had voluntarily given up cow slaughter, they now flaunted it as a religious obligation. Hindus deliberately routed religious processions to pass by mosques, increasing the volume of their music whenever they came within earshot of Moslems at worship. Outbreaks occurred with mounting severity throughout 1924. In September, in Kohat, Mos-

Out of prison after serving two years of a six-year term, Gandhi attends to his correspondence while recuperating by the sea; he came out of prison weighing only ninety pounds.

lems killed 155 Hindus and drove all survivors out of town.

"Hindu-Moslem unity means home rule," Gandhi said. "There is no question more important and more pressing than this." So saying, he announced a fast for twenty-one days.

A Hindu, he chose to fast in the house of Mohammed Ali, his Moslem friend, with a Christian missionary, Charles Freer Andrews, as his nurse. He subsisted entirely on water, reserving the right to add salt as plain water nauseated him. In a series of short messages, he told his followers that instead of working for a change of heart among Englishmen, they must for the moment address themselves to creating a change of heart among Hindus and Moslems. "Before we dare think of freedom we must be brave enough to love one another, to tolerate one another's religion, even prejudices and superstitions." A week after he began fasting, three hundred representatives of the Moslem and Hindu faiths convened a "unity conference" in Delhi. With quickening concern for the health of the Mahatma, they passed a number of resolutions of reconciliation. On the twenty-first day, he broke his fast in a ceremony that included a reading from the Koran and the singing of Christian and Hindu hymns. Sipping some orange juice in the presence of leaders from all three communities, he whispered his injunction to lay down their lives "for the cause of brotherhood."

Gandhi was re-elected president of the Congress in 1925. But he kept himself removed from the factional quarrels that absorbed so many of his colleagues in the central and provincial legislatures. Sadly, he recognized that during his imprisonment the party had reverted to its old ways. Once again it was dominated by the well-to-do, big-city intellectuals under whom the great masses of India's poor stood to fare no better than they did under the British. "Their method is not my method," and so saying, he turned his back on the bulk of educated India and set about building a nation as he had built his movement—"from the bottom up."

Concentrating on his program for constructive service, he spent a year touring the villages. To the thousands who gathered to hear him wherever he stopped, he preached nonviolence, an end to untouchability, and the virtues of *khadi* (homespun). His speeches reverberated with notes of urgency. "India is dying. If you want to save India, do it by doing the little I ask for. I want you to take up the wheel forthwith or perish."

By now he had made the spinning wheel a symbol of freedom through self-help. Not long thereafter he put it in the center of the Congress party flag. Western-educated

Indians could understand his plea that they wear homespun, for this was only the other and necessary side of a movement to boycott British goods. Having been exposed to the virtues of the machine age, however, they saw the spinning wheel as pitifully inefficient and accused Gandhi of misrepresenting its economic importance. In rebuttal Gandhi would patiently explain the facts of peasant life to the privileged. Millions of laborers were landless, he pointed out. Millions more had land to till but were still idle for at least four months out of every year. One-tenth of the population lived on one meal a day and could not earn, on the average, more than three rupees a month. In his judgment, cottage industries clearly offered the best hope for increasing their pitifully low incomes, and of the various cottage industries hand-spinning was the simplest and easiest to accommodate in the average peasant's home. Perhaps, he conceded, the spinning wheel did rank as a modest, low-yield tool. Still, if you were a peasant earning no more than three rupees a month, an additional five or six rupees from the sale of homespun could look like a fortune.

Staying with untouchables wherever he went, he put first things first. "For every rupee spent on these garlands, you could give sixteen women one meal," he reproached the people of one village. Adoring followers would present him with gold and silver boxes. He would auction them off and credit the proceeds to his *khadi* fund. An indefatigable fund raiser, he was able to charm the jewelry off the ears, noses, arms and ankles of every woman in his audience. He would pass among the crowd selling homespun he had made himself, and whenever his train stopped he would thrust his cupped palms out the coach window, begging coins and trinkets of the people waiting on the station platforms. As one of his followers said at the time, "It costs a great deal of money to keep the Mahatma in poverty."

In November, 1927, along with a number of other Indian leaders, Gandhi was summoned to Delhi for a meeting at the viceroy's house. He traveled a thousand miles to be told what could be contained on a postcard: A royal commission, headed by Sir John Simon, was on its way to inquire into India's competence for self-government.

The Reforms Act of 1919, under which India was then being governed, called for a review of the country's constitutional status after ten years. The news that the Conservative party had chosen to conduct the review more than a year in advance was received with understandable suspicion. In Gandhi's mind it could mean only that the Conservatives feared a Labor victory in 1929, in which event an intolerably tolerant view might be taken of India's aspirations for independence. The commission was to be made up entirely of Englishmen and entirely of white men.

Gandhi expressed the prevalent reaction in two succinct sentences: "Freedom is the gift of God. It is not something for any foreign mission to decide."

When "the Simon Seven" arrived, it was met everywhere with black flag demonstrations and shuttered shop windows. Illiterate Indians who knew no other words of English shouted, "Simon, go back," lining the streets by the thousands in nonviolent protest. Mounted police charged into the crowds, flailing out indiscriminately with long, steel-tipped bamboo sticks. When, despite repeated attacks, the people did not strike back, Gandhi was persuaded to resume *Satyagraha* where he had suspended it six years earlier, in Bardoli. On his instructions, the peasants there refused to pay a twenty-two per cent increase in taxes. Although the government jailed hundreds and confiscated their farms, the people stood fast. A sympathy strike in June brought contributions from all parts of the country.

Two months later the British capitulated, canceling the tax increase and returning the confiscated properties.

India seethed. The next year and a half there were frequent strikes and sporadic outbursts of violence. Within the Congress party full independence became an issue that pitted Jawaharlal Nehru against his father, the author of a parliamentary scheme proposing dominion status. Pressed to choose between them, Gandhi agreed to lead a fight for full independence if dominion status had not been granted by December, 1929.

A year later, forty-year-old Jawaharlal was president of the Congress and India was still a colony. True to his word, Gandhi urged passage of a resolution calling for total independence and secession from the empire. A grim but excited assembly then instructed him to lead the country into civil disobedience.

On December 31, 1929, in an act that struck the British as seditious but the Indians as a living resolution for the new year, Congress members gathered on the banks of the Ravi and unfurled the flag of independence. Afterward, while the country waited for the signal that would launch that rebellion, Gandhi withdrew to his *ashram* hut to think. His declaration of January 26 as "Independence Day" helped the suspense only momentarily. How, where, and against what British-made injustice the first attack would be launched was not revealed fully until March 2. Then in a long letter to the viceroy, he laid out his whole plan:

"Dear Friend:

"Before embarking on civil disobedience and taking the risk I have dreaded to take all these years, I would fain approach you and find a way out. . . . Though I hold the British rule in India to be a curse, I do not . . . consider Englishmen in general to be worse than any other people on earth. . . Indeed much that I have learnt of the evil of British rule is due to the writings of frank and courageous Englishmen who have not hesitated to tell the unpalatable truth about that rule . . . And why do I regard the British rule as a curse? It has impoverished the dumb millions by a system of progressive exploitation and by ruinous, expensive military and civil administration which the country can never afford. It has reduced us politically to serfdom. It has sapped the foundations of our culture.

"Nothing but organized nonviolence can check the organized violence of the British government . . . I know that in embarking on nonviolence, I shall be running what

141

might be fairly termed a mad risk, but the victories of truth have never been won without risks, often of the greatest character."

Gandhi then went on to specify his demands: Reduce the land revenue, military expenditures, and government salaries by fifty per cent; discharge all political prisoners; enforce the constitutional guarantees of freedom of expression; and, finally, abolish the salt laws which prevented villages from using their own local salt. "I respectfully invite you to pave the way for the immediate removal of these evils, and thus open the way for a real conference between equals.

"But," Gandhi went on, "if my letter makes no appeal to your heart, on the eleventh day of this month I shall proceed, with such co-workers of the *ashram* as I can take, to disregard the provisions of the salt laws."

The salt laws? Nehru and other high-born members of Congress were as astonished as the British by Gandhi's choice for the prime target. Salt manufacture was confined to the seacoast and employed the most politically backward people in the country. Even if Gandhi were successful in organizing a strike, most old-style Congress leaders were at a loss to understand how the impact could possibly be big enough to set off a revolution.

But Gandhi knew his terrain. The British government held a monopoly on salt. It was against the law to make it or to buy it from any other source. Furthermore, the government imposed a tax on salt that was particularly burdensome to the peasants. Salt was the one thing that the poor man used more than the rich man. His daily requirements were more because he perspired more; he worked in sun-scorched fields, in a climate where ninety degrees is considered too cold for swimming. For the average peasant, the annual tax was equivalent to three days' income. In a few weeks the intellectuals would come to understand what the peasants had known instinctively—that in a grain of salt Gandhi had found the perfect symbol of freedom. To oppose the salt laws would be to assert a simple, elementary human right.

On the Salt March to Dandi. Marching beside Gandhi is Mrs. Sarojini Naidu, first woman president of the Indian National Congress. Note the indispensable pocket watch. Although noted for his patience, Gandhi could not tolerate the waste of time. To him, one minute's delay in the start of a demonstration meant that freedom would be one minute later coming to India.

Lord Irwin, the viceroy, replied through a secretary. He expressed regret at Mr. Gandhi's proposed course but considered the government's policies in India non-negotiable.

"On bended knee I asked for bread," said Gandhi. "I received a stone instead."

At six-thirty on the morning of March 12, 1930, Gandhi took his place at the head of a column of seventy-eight *ashram* members and began his famous Salt March. His destination was Dandi, two hundred and forty miles due south

143

on the Arabian Sea. Among the marchers were scholars and untouchables. The Mahatma, at sixty, was the oldest. The youngest was a boy of sixteen. For the convenience of the British police, the name and record of each participant was published in the official *Satyagraha* journal, *Young India*.

They marched for twenty-four days and as they advanced thousands arrived from all over India to join them. Unfailingly cheerful, Gandhi set a pace that his footsore followers had a hard time maintaining. He considered child's play anything less than twelve miles a day. He rose as usual at 4 A.M. for his morning prayers. While the ranks were resting or sleeping, he was out making speeches to villagers, attending to his correspondence, or writing articles for the press.

"Watch," Gandhi had said. "I will give a signal to the nation." Uneasily, the world watched. On the night of April 5, the marchers reached the Dandi beach. "God willing," Gandhi announced, "I expect with my companions to commence actual civil disobedience at 6:30 in the morning." At sunrise, having spent most of the night in prayer, he walked into the sea, then, returning to shore, picked up some salt left from evaporated seawater.

The effect was electric. Suddenly, all over India, salt became a mysterious word, "a word of power," as Nehru put it. "It seemed as though a spring had been released." India's long seacoast was lined with peasants squatting on the beaches unlawfully scooping salt into pans. In Bombay, Congress party members converted the roof of their headquarters into a salt factory. There and in the other big cities, well-to-do citizens fought for the privilege of buying it. The salt that Gandhi had picked up on the Dandi beach went at auction for more than one hundred dollars.

Challenged, the Government ordered mass arrests and reinvoked censorship. One by one, Gandhi's most prominent disciples were picked up and sentenced from six months to two years on various charges of sedition, among them Jawaharal Nehru and the mayor of Calcutta. Within a month, according to official records, the viceroy filled the jails with no less than sixty thousand political offenders.

Incredibly, although the British action provoked *hartals* and in one incident on the northwest frontier government troops killed seventy demonstrators, the *Satyagrahis* remained stubbornly nonviolent. The boycott of foreign cloth became almost universal, many Indians quit their government jobs, many more refused to pay taxes, and all over the country women from aristocratic and middle-class homes marched on picket lines protesting the sale of English textiles.

From his camp near Dandi, Gandhi issued orders to his freedom fighters, talked with foreign correspondents, and watched for fresh opportunities to win world opinion. "God willing," he announced toward the end of April, he would next lead the *Satyagrahis* on a raid of the salt depots at Dharsana, one hundred and fifty miles north of Bombay. This was too much for the British. In the middle of the night of May 4, thirty armed policemen and two officers, accompanied by a magistrate, appeared at his campsite and took him off to jail. This time, having no intention of providing him with another platform, the British bypassed the courts and scarcely took the trouble to file charges. He was held under an obscure hundred-year-old regulation that let the state detain persons without trial.

His arrest only served to focus world opinion on the Dharsana salt works. In his absence, plans for the raid went forward under the leadership of Mrs. Sarojini Naidu, a famous poet; Imam Sahib, an elderly inmate of the *ashram;* and Gandhi's second son, Manilal. On May 21, a column of more than two hundred *Satyagrahis,* headed by Manilal, advanced on the great salt pans. Facing them were four hundred Surat policemen, commanded by six British officers. Between them were ditches and barbed wire. What happened a few moments later was made known throughout the civilized world by such eye witnesses as Webb Miller of the United Press:

"Suddenly, at a word of command scores of native policemen rushed upon the advancing marchers and rained blows on their heads with their steel-shod *lathis* (sticks). Not one of the marchers even raised an arm to fend off the blows.

The power of nonviolence was demonstrated throughout India as Gandhi's campaign of civil disobedience gathered momentum. Here a group of his followers sit passively while British police flail at them with clubs.

They went down like tenpins. From where I stood I heard the sickening whack of the clubs on unprotected skulls. . . . Those struck down fell sprawling, unconscious or writhing with fractured skulls or broken shoulders . . . The survivors, without breaking ranks, silently and doggedly marched on until struck down."

The marchers came in waves, one column succeeding another. "Although everyone knew that within a few minutes he would be beaten down, perhaps killed, I could detect no sign of wavering or fear. They marched steadily, with

heads up, without the encouragement of music or cheering
or any possibility that they might escape injury or death.
The police rushed out and methodically and mechanically
beat them down. There was no fight, no struggle. Hour after
hour, stretcher bearers carried back a stream of inert, bleeding men."

The raids and beatings continued for several days. Miller
reported: "In no case did I see a volunteer—all told there
were two thousand, five hundred of them—even raise an
arm to deflect the blows. Obviously it was their purpose to
force the police to beat them. . . . In eighteen years of report-
ing in twenty-two countries, I have never witnessed such

harrowing scenes as at Dharsana. The western mind can grasp violence returned by violence, can understand a fight, but is, I've found, perplexed and baffled by the sight of men advancing coldly and deliberately and submitting to beating without attempting defense . . . It seemed that they were thoroughly imbued with Gandhi's nonviolence creed, and the leaders constantly stood in front of the ranks imploring them to remember that Gandhi's soul was with them."

Nonviolence similarly ruled throughout the country. Thousands of *Satyagrahis*, including the warlike Sikhs, marched through the streets carrying red, green and white banners, singing "We will take *swaraj*—India our motherland." At other times they simply stood imperturbably in silent phalanxes, daring the police to strike them. In prison, Gandhi was particularly heartened by news from the northwest frontier that hundreds of thousands of fierce Moslem Pathans had stood firm even in the face of machine-gun fire.

The Mahatma's power was unlike anything Westerners had ever seen before. In jail now were at least a hundred thousand voluntary prisoners, including twelve thousand Moslems. There were not enough jails to hold the thousands more who clamored to join them. The country faced economic paralysis, and the rest of the world watched in horror, fearful that in the impending chaos there might be another and bloodier Amritsar. Urging his countrymen to face facts, the *London Daily Herald* correspondent wrote: "Incalculable disaster may yet be avoided by the frank recognition that the imprisoned Mahatma now incarnates the very soul of India."

It was apparent that if the British were not violent they would lose, and if they were violent they would lose anyway. For European readers, the poet Tagore accurately described the Salt March achievement in terms of Britain's lost moral prestige. Writing in the *Manchester Guardian*, he said: "Even though Asia is physically weak and unable to protect herself from aggression where her vital interests are menaced, she can now afford to look down on Europe where before she looked up." Though it was to be seventeen years before

India became formally independent, freedom for India was inevitable from the moment Gandhi stooped on the beach at Dandi for a handful of salt.

One of the few British leaders who failed to recognize this fact was a Conservative member of parliament named Winston Churchill.

For the next eight months, during which the Mahatma caught up on his rest in Yeravda jail, official Britain was preoccupied with the question: "What to do about Gandhi?" The Prime Minister, Ramsay MacDonald, was virtually overwhelmed with telegrams, all of them demanding the Mahatma's release. During the summer the report of the Simon Commission was received. The first Round Table Conference to consider its recommendations was held in London from November 12, 1930, to January 19, 1931; its main accomplishment was to schedule a second conference. The only Indians in attendance were the viceroy's appointees, all of whom seemed of a mind to oblige the British with reasonable explanations for inaction.

Meanwhile the Conservatives in Parliament, led by Winston Churchill, were eager to put an end to any considerations of independence. "We ought to make it perfectly clear," Churchill said, "that we intend to remain rulers of India for a very long and indefinite period, and though we welcome cooperation from loyal Indians we will have no truck with lawlessness and treason." Gandhism, as he called it, "will have to be crushed."

To the viceroy in Delhi, such talk seemed beside the point. The All-India Congress Working Committee had extended the scope of civil disobedience to include non-payment of cow taxes and the boycott of foreign cloth, banks, shipping, and insurance companies. "Gandhism" not only had frustrated his attempts to maintain law and order but had precipitated a serious drop in revenue. Thus, before the year was out, both he and the Prime Minister were inclined to be conciliatory—so much so that in his farewell remarks to the Round Table Conference, MacDonald said he hoped that

Congress members would be among the delegates when the group reassembled.

Six days later, Lord Irwin unconditionally released Gandhi and twenty other Congress leaders, including both Nehrus. Almost immediately Gandhi wrote Irwin for an interview, which was promptly granted. Beginning on February 17, there ensued a series of eight meetings, during which Gandhi and the viceroy talked for a total of twenty-four hours. In London, Winston Churchill attacked the negotiations with undisguised fury. "It is alarming," he said, "and also nauseating to see Mr. Gandhi, a seditious, Middle Temple lawyer now posing as a fakir of a type well known in the East, striding half-naked up the steps of the Viceregal Palace while he is still organizing and conducting a defiant campaign of civil disobedience, to parlay on equal terms with the representative of the King-Emperor."

On March 5, 1931, Gandhi and Lord Irwin signed a pact that was noteworthy more as the basis for future negotiations than as a statement of reconciliation. The Government agreed to release all nonviolent prisoners, to recognize the boycott of foreign cloth as a legitimate right, to restore all confiscated property, and—most significantly—to withdraw the ban on making salt at home. Gandhi agreed to suspend his civil disobedience and to attend the second Round Table Conference, which was scheduled to convene in London that fall.

But the pact promised neither independence nor dominion status, and before many weeks had gone by Gandhi was being roundly criticized for having accepted terms short of the complete self-government for which he had pledged "ceaseless civil disobedience." He could explain his seeming inconsistency only in terms of *Satyagraha*. "There comes a stage when the *Satyagrahi* may no longer refuse to negotiate with his opponent. His object is always to convert his opponent by love."

In August, he sailed for London. The forthcoming con-

Free once more, after eight months in prison in Poona, Gandhi acknowledges the cheers of the Bombay crowds that greeted him in January, 1931.

ference promised to yield few specific gains for India but for both parties it offered magnificent opportunities for propaganda. On the propaganda front, it was a complete victory for Gandhi.

Still photographers, newsreel cameramen, and foreign correspondents followed him everywhere. Aboard ship, he was photographed, sometimes in the company of his goat, spinning on his collapsible wheel; participating in lifeboat drills; playing on deck with child passengers; visiting the captain on the bridge. The press made much of the fact that his party had chosen to travel in the lowest class, as deck passengers. On the second day at sea, it was reported, he had been shocked to see the amount of luggage brought aboard by several aides. At the first stopover port, he ordered seven suitcases and a trunk sent back.

In London, he turned down invitations from the well-to-do and instead took a small room in the slums. From there he traveled widely, speaking informally to groups large and small, always with the same message: the need to forge "an honorable partnership" between Britain and India. He had private conferences with intellectual and political leaders but he insisted that his energies could be better spent cultivating the workers. "The impression I make on them will percolate upwards," he said. With some apprehension, his friends watched him move into Lancashire, an industrial community that had been particularly hard hit by the Indian boycott of English cloth. Amazingly, Gandhi was able to convert the fact of their unemployment into a telling example of the gross disparity between British and Indian labor. "Tell me," he asked the working class of Lancashire, "what I am to do with a fifth of the human race living on the verge of starvation? . . . You have three million unemployed. We have nearly three hundred million unemployed, or underemployed for half the year. Your average *dole* is seventy shillings. Our average *income* is seven shillings sixpence a month." To the daily distress of the Conservatives, the British press carried photograph after photograph of workers cheering Gandhi and crowding around him for a

At the 1931 Round Table, St. James's Palace, London. To his right: British Prime Minister Ramsay MacDonald.

153

chance to shake his hand. "If I was in India," one of the Lancashire workers was quoted as saying, "I would say the same thing that Mr. Gandhi is saying. We understand each other now."

His highly publicized three-months stay was marked by a spirit of sincerity, gaiety, and simplicity that the British public found irresistible. When a reporter commented on the unorthodoxy of his clothing, he said: "You British have your plus fours," referring to the droopy knickers that the then Prince of Wales had made fashionable. "These are my minus fours." After attending a reception at Buckingham Palace, a reporter asked him if he had found a shawl, loincloth, and sandals sufficient clothing for the occasion. "The King had enough on for both of us," he replied.

But lest the world misinterpret the general cordiality, Winston Churchill made it clear that in the minds of Britain's ruling class, Gandhi's ideas were still politically unacceptable. Churchill refused to see him. It soon became clear, too, that the liberal disposition of Ramsay MacDonald's labor government was not to prevail. The MacDonald government was replaced by a coalition including Conservatives, Lord Irwin was replaced with an unsympathetic viceroy, and there was a perceptible hardening of London's attitude toward Indian nationalism, even before the talks began.

After ten weeks, the discussion ended with no issues resolved and with a general impression, widely encouraged by Mr. Churchill, that the Indians were too divided to be trusted with self-government. Gandhi called the Conference "an utter failure" and announced that he had now no choice but to "go back and invite the nation to a course of suffering."

Exactly one week after his return, Gandhi was back in jail. India's new viceroy, Lord Willingdon, had launched plans to crush the Congress party even as His Majesty's representatives in St. James Palace were speaking of "cooperation" and "the new partnership." Declaring the Congress "an unlawful association," he reinvoked censorship and moved summarily to arrest all the party's leaders. Gandhi was seized with members of the Congress Working Committee on January 4, 1932. Once again he was lodged in Yeravda prison.

For almost a year thereafter the Indian landscape was rocked with violence. Demonstrations of civil disobedience, *lathi* charges, and mass arrests followed one after another in almost predictable sequence. By October, more than sixty thousand convictions were recorded for "subversive" political activities.

Meanwhile, the British announced provisions for a new constitution for India. For some time the law had provided that in provincial elections Hindus vote only for Hindus and Moslems only for Moslems. Now it was proposed that a separate electorate also be established for Hindu untouchables. The British had not initiated the idea. The untouchables themselves, under the leadership of the well-educated, tough-minded Dr. Bhimrao Ramjo Ambedkar, had been advocating the same thing. Ironically, their awakening ambitions and the cold practicality of British policy were forging a natural conspiracy that threatened to make Gandhi's cherished goal of unification virtually hopeless. He reacted passionately. "I would far rather that Hinduism died than that untouchability lived," he said.

On September 20, he began "a fast unto the death." Henceforth, he announced from his prison cell, his life would be in the hands of the *Harijans,* the untouchables, "the children of God." He would not eat again until the *Harijans* and other Hindus had come together in a single political unit.

Although Ambedkar called the fast "a political stunt," everyone who knew Gandhi was confident that he would do precisely what he said. To keep him alive, a hastily assembled conference of Hindu leaders went to work feverishly on a plan that both the British and the untouchables would accept. "At first," Nehru recalled some years later, "I felt angry with him in his religious and sentimental approach to a political question . . . then came news of a magic wave of enthusiasm running through Hindu society. Untouchability appeared to be doomed. What a magician, I thought, was this little man sitting in Yeravda prison, and how well he knew how to pull the strings that moved people's hearts!"

Weakened by his imprisonment, Gandhi's body began to waste rapidly by the third day. He could hardly move without being nauseated, he had to be moved to the bathroom on a stretcher, he was unable to take water, and he was afflicted by sharp, racking pains. On the fourth day, his blood pressure was alarmingly high and prison physicians considered his condition serious.

But by the end of that day, Hindus and *Harijans* had drafted a pact to which Gandhi was able to whisper his approval. Essentially, it provided for one unified electorate but for a much higher representation for the *Harijans* than they would have had under the proposal for a separate electorate. Twenty-four hours later, word came from Ten Downing Street that the agreement was acceptable to the Prime Minister. At 5:15 on the afternoon of the sixth day, Kasturbai handed Gandhi a glass of orange juice and the fast was broken.

To make it clear that what had happened was more than a momentary act of political grace, a large representative congress of Hindus resolved, "Henceforth no one shall be regarded as untouchable," and promised to make "equality by law" the first act of the *Swaraj* parliament. But in Gandhi's total war against untouchability, this constituted a bare beginning. From his jail cell, he now proceeded to direct a relentless campaign of social reform in which untouchability figured as the central evil, the symbol of all the social problems—poverty, illiteracy, caste, unemployment—that Indians must vow to correct if, in his opinion, they were to be worthy of the freedom they demanded of the British. Regularly from his cell there issued a series of press statements. He founded a weekly paper, *Harijan,* and through its columns urged Hindus to open all temples, wells, roads, and schools to the depressed classes.

When in May of 1933 news reached him of backsliding at the Sabarmati *ashram,* he embarked on a twenty-one-day fast as a way of reminding his followers that he was indeed in earnest. Alarmed, fearing the consequences if he were to die in their custody, the British released him on the first day. For the next three weeks, subsisting largely on Vichy water, he lay on a cot in the home of a wealthy disciple, Lady Vittal das Thackersey, much of the time in a semi-coma. Though he developed jaundice and went from ninety-nine to eighty pounds, he endured the ordeal surprisingly well.

In August, suspecting that he was plotting a resumption of massive civil disobedience, Lord Willingdon had him again arrested, only to release him three days later on condition that he confine himself to Poona City. He defied the order, so the authorities promptly slapped him back in jail. When they compounded his punishment by cutting off all communications with his lieutenants, he began another fast. The viceroy then released him, with the implicit understanding that for the balance of his year's sentence he would not engage in civil disobedience.

Gandhi now entered what some foreign correspondents repeatedly and mistakenly called "one of his quiet periods." For the next six years, he kept out of jail, his remarks about British rule were more prophetic than revolutionary, and though the Congress party hardly made a move without consulting him first, his voice on public issues was distinctly muted. But he was hardly quiet. He merely began to speak more as a teacher and less as a politician. His mission was to prove that, even in the most primitive villages, a decent community could be built through nonviolence.

In September, 1933, he gave Sabarmati *ashram* to a society of untouchables and moved to Wardha, a small town whose chief distinction was that it lay almost precisely in the geographical center of the continent. Two months later he set out on a ten-month tour, traveling, all told, nearly 12,500 miles. He visited remote settlements where no national leader had ever been seen before and, sometimes merely by shaking hands with untouchables, violated taboos that had been held for centuries. Toward the end of the tour, while on his way to the Municipal Hall in Poona, he narrowly escaped injury from an exploding bomb. But no organized opposition could stop him. He returned to Wardha with a total of 800,000 rupees for his *Harijan* fund.

In 1935, he built his model village. As if determined to prove that good communities could emerge from the most unlikely environments, he deliberately chose a site in the poorest section of India, a few miles from Wardha, inhabited entirely by peasants, three-fourths of whom were outcastes. Here he founded Sevagram ("service village").

For the rest of his life Sevagram was home. In time it became the spiritual capital of India, attracting thousands of visitors from all parts of the world, the young and the old, the rich and the poor, the learned and unlearned, the

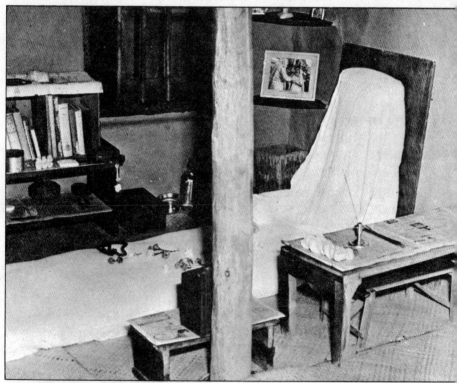

The Mahatma's room in the ashram at Sevagram, Wardha, his home from 1935 on. On the top shelf near his books stand the symbolic three little monkeys: "Hear no evil, see no evil, speak no evil."

strong and the weak, authentic geniuses and known crack-
pots. To all alike, he was simple, direct, and friendly. And
to all he presented a living lesson in simplicity. His hut,
made of mud and bamboo, had no electricity. The three-by-
eight-foot living room was furnished with a small writing
table, a wastepaper basket, a spinning wheel, a straw mat,
a board that he used as a prop for his back, and two shelves
of about a dozen books, including *The Gita* and *The Gospel
of St. John*. He kept a paperweight inscribed, "God is love,"
and a cheap figurine of the three monkeys, "Hear no evil,
see no evil, speak no evil." On one wall hung a picture of
Jesus, on another a motto: "When you are in the right, you
can afford to keep your temper, and when you are in the
wrong, you cannot afford to lose it." Besides his clothing—
which was minimal—his only worldly goods consisted of a
dollar pocket watch, two food bowls, a water pitcher, several
fountain pens, some stationery, and a pair of spectacles.

The quality of his ministry was perhaps best symbolized
by an enormous window that dominated the entrance of his
hut. It was as if he were inviting the whole population to
look in on him. Now in his late sixties, he was Bapu (father)
to all India, consulted as much on matters of domestic relations ("Bapu, shall I divorce my wife?") as on matters of
state. Sometimes, to the annoyance of Congress leaders, he
seemed to give more attention to the personal problems of
the peasants than he did to problems of politics.

The secret of his enormous appeal was not merely that
he listened to others. It was also in his readiness to talk
honestly about himself. He discussed his fears, doubts, and
worries openly and without embarrassment. He spoke can-
didly of sex and personal hygiene. He confessed naturally
to feelings that most people in that post-Victorian age kept
resolutely repressed. He touched almost everybody at the
level of the secret self and he had the powerful effect of
making them feel less alone, less inferior, more important,
and somehow more aware of their potential as human beings.

Despite his seemingly leisurely and sympathetic way with
visitors, he was acutely conscious of the need to make the

most of his time. To get away from interviewers and admirers, he made it a habit to observe one full day of silence every week, usually on Mondays. One reason that he was able to accommodate so many people during his day was simply that he wasted so few of his hours eating or sleeping. He customarily ate only five items of food a day—goat's milk, some nuts, a bit of fruit. Routinely, he arose at 4 A.M. One of his minor failures was that he was never able to inculcate in his followers a similar respect for the clock. "I think *swaraj* will also be delayed by forty-five minutes," he was prone to say whenever a meeting was delayed by latecomers.

Sevagram operated as an educational community, based on theories that had much in common with those of the famous American philosopher, John Dewey. It was a community, moreover, that was devoted not only to the progressive education of its residents but, by example, to the education of all Indians, be they peasants or policymakers. What Gandhi did at Sevagram was directly addressed to India's seemingly insoluble problems of urbanization and overpopulation—the same problems that thirty years later were to dominate the minds of statesmen in even so affluent a country as America.

During the thirties, India's population was increasing at the rate of five million a year. The big cities were swelling disproportionately as millions of young men, seeing no future in farming, flocked to the ghettos of Calcutta and Bombay. Although Gandhi did not rule out artificial methods of birth control, he advocated self-control and late marriages (no earlier than twenty-one for women and the mid-twenties for men) as being more workable among Indians, since neither cost any money. He promoted economic diversification as the only way of providing villages with incomes that would keep young people alive and in the villages. The spinning wheel came to be understood more and more as the symbol of British exploitation. At the same time, his attachment to the land continued to express itself through the promotion of agricultural experiments. "To forget how to dig the earth," he said, "is to forget ourselves."

160

His ideas of education were astonishingly modern, grounded as they were in the Dewey principle of learning by doing. The purpose of what he called his "new education" was the achievement of a "just social order in which there is no unnatural division between the haves and the have-nots and everybody is assured a living wage and a right to freedom." Outlining the objectives of his village school, he said that its curriculum would be properly concerned with all aspects of village life, from "the moment a child is conceived until the moment of death"—an idea that sounds amazingly close to the "cradle-to-grave" approach so popular among American educators today.

A strengthening of village government lay at the heart of his program for community development. Increased concentration of power in the big cities, he maintained, would ultimately lead to massive breakdowns in public services and to the psychological separation not merely between the powerful and the powerless, not merely between men and nature, but ultimately between man and his Self. He sought nothing less than to decentralize this power among the 700,000 villages of India. Though he hardly got beyond the planning stage, he spelled out proposals for coping constructively with urban growth that as the years went by were to gain relevance far beyond the boundaries of India. He wanted to see each village organized as "a complete republic, independent of its neighbors for its own vital wants, yet interdependent for many others in which dependence is a necessity. . . . As far as possible, every activity will be conducted on the cooperative basis. Government of the village will be conducted by the Panchayat, of five persons anually elected by the adult villagers, male and female, possessing minimum prescribed qualifications . . ." He insisted that, whereas self-rule in the big cities might have to wait on independence, the only things that held it back in the villages were poverty, illiteracy, and the absence of will. The British would not interfere, he maintained, for at the village level the Crown's "sole effective connection was the exaction of revenue."

TWELVE

Freedom

Abruptly, the Mahatma's preoccupation with community development came to an end. World events forced a re-emergence of Gandhi the politician.

On September 3, 1939, England went to war with Germany. A few hours later, without bothering to consult India's leaders, the viceroy declared that India too was at war.

His arbitrary action outraged Indians of all faiths and all political persuasions. Gandhi's response, however, was more sad than angry. Within twenty-four hours he was on a train to Simlak, the summer capital, to convey his sympathy "with England and France from the purely humanitarian standpoint." In the midst of his interview with Lord Linlithgow, the viceroy, he began to weep, overcome by the thought that the Houses of Parliament and Westminster Abbey might be destroyed. He wept for "the idea of England." As he explained later to the readers of *Harijan*, he also wept because "in the secret of my heart I am in perpetual quarrel with God that He should allow such things to go on."

There were times when it took all his strength to resist concluding that his life had been wasted. Throughout the thirties, sensing an approaching holocaust in the actions of Hitler and Mussolini, he had systematically espoused non-

This photograph taken at a 1940 Congress Committee meeting in Allahabad, India, is unusual on two accounts. The Mahatma, busily at work, is unaware his picture is being taken; the photographer who caught him off guard was India's future prime minister, Nehru.

violent response to military aggression. When Italy overran Abyssinia, he had advised Emperor Haile Selassie not to seek help from stronger nations but to undertake positive, nonviolent resistance. When the Nazis began to herd Jews into gas chambers, he had urged voluntary sacrifice. "I can conceive the necessity for the immolation of hundreds, if not thousands, to appease the hunger of dictators."

Now the effectiveness of nonviolence was being tested against a conscienceless and brazenly immoral Adolph Hitler. As a consequence, the judgment was being made everywhere that nonviolence as a weapon worked only when the opponent was civilized. There were times when Gandhi could almost agree. "Nonviolence seems almost impotent," he said. Still, he did not falter. Though men rejected nonviolence, violence offered no hopeful alternative, for vio-

163

lence only begat more violence. Resolving his doubts in prayer, he declared "that neither God nor nonviolence is impotent. Impotence is in men."

Though he declared himself anti-Nazi, he could not bring himself to endorse warfare. To critics who reminded him of his position during World War I, he said, "My aim is not to be consistent with my previous statements, but to be consistent with the truth." To Nehru and the other Congress leaders, he urged a policy of unconditional moral support for the Allies, limited by strict adherence to the precepts of nonviolence.

But the Indian National Congress was not a party of pacifists. With few exceptions, leaders of the Congress had pursued *ahimsa* for the very practical reason that, since India had no arms, nonviolence seemed to be the only practical course. For many, lip service to *Satyagraha* was simply the price of Gandhi's leadership, and they needed Gandhi. But with the advent of war, they readily declared their willingness to abandon nonviolence—indeed, to back the war with every resource at their command if Britain would only grant independence.

In the summer of 1940, after France's surrender to the Nazis and Britain's retreat from Dunkirk, the Congress Working Committee did just that, offering, in addition, to enter into a provisional government for the better prosecution of the war. For Gandhi, this position was intolerable. Henceforth, he told the committee, "You will have to do your best without me."

But it soon became clear that Winston Churchill, Britain's new Prime Minister, was of no mind to bargain. As he was to say in a classic speech in Parliament in 1942, he had not become the King's first minister "in order to preside at the liquidation of the British Empire." Congress' offer, therefore, was forcefully rejected, the stated reason being that to approve a government led by the Congress would be to jeopardize the welfare of the Moslems. Stunned by the rebuff, Congress withdrew its resolution of support and asked Gandhi to take charge again. He accepted their invitation but resisted firmly all pressure to mount a disruptive program of civil disobedience.

In December, British-Indian relations took a dramatic turn. Joining the Nazis, the Japanese attacked Pearl Harbor, bringing the United States into the war on the side of the Allies. The effect was to magnify all the issues centering on colonialism and to activate every faction into frenzied, sometimes hysterical, campaigns. There were those who pushed for renewed negotiations, on the assumption that even Winston Churchill would have to acknowledge that simply by proffering or withholding its cooperation, India was now in a pivotal position to affect the war in the Pacific. Others, less of a mind to invest their faith in a change in Churchill, were counting on the United States to help them press Britain into an unconditional promise of independence. At the extremes were those who agitated for an armed insurrection against the British and those who advocated active collaboration with the Japanese.

By early 1942, the Japanese issue was critical. Having made a lightning-swift sweep through southeast Asia, Japanese troops stood at the very borders of India, poised for an invasion. At the same time, news came that a one-time firebrand of the Congress Party, Subhas Chandra Bose, had escaped from British custody in Calcutta and was reported to be either in Tokyo or Singapore actively organizing an Indian national army to march alongside the Japanese. The country was thrust into a perilous state of suspense. Though divided in their reactions to Bose and the Japanese, the people seemed almost unanimous in their hostility toward England. "Never," reported the viceroy, "has India been as anti-British as it is today."

As was by now his predictable response whenever the people's feelings were about to boil over, Gandhi met the crisis with a series of policy statements, each as logical as a lawyer's brief, through which he gradually raised the debate to a moral plane. To those who would turn against Britain when she was down, he said merely, "We do not seek our independence out of Britain's ruin." To those who were tempted to regard the Japanese as saviors, he said firmly that India's independence would never be found in an exchange of Western for Asian imperialism. Should the Japanese actually invade India, nonviolence should be the Indian recourse. "Neither food nor shelter is to be given them," he said in June, 1942, "nor any dealings to be established with them. They should be made to feel that they are not wanted."

But he also decided that only a free India could effectively resist the Japanese; whatever the risk, the British would have to quit India.

Before resorting to his ultimate weapon, massive civil disobedience, he asked President Franklin Roosevelt to intervene. "If my demands are just," he wrote Roosevelt, "America can insist on Indian independence before supplying the British with weapons . . . Since America has become the predominant partner in the Allied cause, she is partner also in Britain's guilt."

President Roosevelt did not go so far as to threaten Churchill with withdrawal of U.S. assistance. He was, however, instrumental in persuading Churchill to send Sir Stafford Cripps to India to negotiate with the Congress party.

The Cripps mission was doomed to failure for two simple reasons: Churchill would not grant full independence, and the Congress would not accept anything less.

Gandhi now was left with no choice but to declare open, nonviolent rebellion against the British. On August 8, he appeared before delegates at the Congress meeting in Bombay and was given the power to initiate civil disobedience at whatever time and by whatever plan he thought strategically desirable. Still hoping to find a basis for compromise, he said that his first act would be to present to the viceroy a new statement of Congress' terms for Indian independence. The delegates, however, should not wait on a reply. "Every one of you," he instructed, "should from this very moment act as if you are free and no longer under the heel of imperialism."

But Lord Linlithgow was under orders to enter into no

Indian newsmen, interviewing Gandhi and Sir Stafford Cripps, Churchill's special emissary to India in 1942, found the Mahatma, as usual, friendly and amusing. Cripps, sent to win nationalist support in the fight against Japan, failed in his mission.

By 1945 Gandhi was indisputably the most public figure in the world. Here he emerges from an interview with H.E. the Viceroy.

talks with "the half naked . . . seditionist." Jail was the place for Gandhi and it was his business to put him there. Before sunrise of August 9, his secret police seized Gandhi, Nehru, and scores of other top-ranking Congressmen. The charge was treason.

The masses received the news of the Mahatma's arrest as if it were a signal for revolt. For weeks riots took place as if in a chain reaction. British officials were murdered, government buildings were set afire, railways and telegraph lines were destroyed. The viceroy publicly accused Gandhi of having triggered the violence. Gandhi, who was held incommunicado, had no opportunity for rebuttal except through personal letters, which the government was careful to suppress. For months he lived in a state of towering indignation and resentment, as every day came reports of fresh uprisings and merciless retaliation by the British military. On ten occasions, troops fired on mobs in Bombay; official records documented a total of five hundred separate military engagements against unarmed Indians.

Early in 1943, despite official reassurances of an adequate food supply, famine in Bengal took the lives of more than a million and a half people. Half sick from grief and frustration, Gandhi was now moved to protest in the only way he could. He began a twenty-one-day fast. This time, he had several targets. One was Lord Linlithgow, from whom he hoped to win a retraction of the charges that he had precipitated the violence. One was his own countrymen, whom he hoped thus to remind of their *Satyagraha* pledge. A third was the democracies among Britain's wartime allies, before whom he meant to dramatize a paradox: that Englishmen who would die for their own freedom would not even grant Indians the right to fight for theirs. The government turned a deaf ear to entreaties that he be pardoned. (Said the famous playwright, George Bernard Shaw: "The King should release Mr. Gandhi unconditionally as an act of grace, unconnected with policy, and apologize for the mental defectiveness of his Cabinet.") To the viceroy, who apparently was determined to appear as tough as Winston Churchill, the fast was "political blackmail." On the twelfth day, Gandhi's pulse was barely perceptible. His doctors reported him to be "very near death." The government acknowledged this report by telling the press that should Gandhi die, it would fly the Union Jack at half-mast.

Amazingly, Gandhi lived.

All told, the British held him, without trial, for six hundred and thirty days. With him, in the beginning, were his two dearest companions, his wife Kasturbai, and his secretary of twenty-five years, Mahadev Desai. But within a week after his imprisonment, Desai dropped dead, apparently from the strain of overwork. Then, late in 1943, Kasturbai fell seriously ill. On February 22, 1944, she died with her head in Gandhi's lap. Her last spoken wish was that she be cremated in a *sari* made from yarn that he had spun. They had been married sixty-two years.

Six weeks later, Gandhi succumbed to an attack of malaria so severe he was delirious. All over the world came renewed demands that he be released. By now India had a new viceroy, Lord Wavell; on May 6, he freed Gandhi, "solely on medical grounds."

By 1944 most Englishmen were convinced that England could no longer morally justify its hold on India. Contemplating the intensity of the 1942 uprising, they had begun to wonder, too, how much longer they might justify the economic cost of holding India by force. In London, there was a strong undercurrent of criticism against the Churchill government for the failure of the Cripps mission. More and more, contending politicians put self-government for India at the top of Britain's postwar agenda.

But what would India be without Britain? This was the question that now came to be Gandhi's consuming concern. His goal had never been merely to get rid of the British. Nor had it been merely to install a government of Indians. Throughout his career he had worked for a *unified* India, a secular state governed by wise and tolerant men committed to the ideals of justice and equality, free of the prejudices of religion and caste. He had, in short, dreamed of a government that would function according to the principles of *Satyagraha*, that would provide a new model for civilized society. This was to be India's special contribution to the world—a crowning testimonal to the validity of nonviolence and the power of peaceful cooperation.

Now, recuperating at the beach near Bombay, listening to daily reports of rioting and mutiny, he began to feel that independence might come too soon. The enemy, it appeared, was no longer the British but the Moslem League. Against his dream of one indivisible nation now stood the League's unyielding demand for a separate Moslem state.

To prevent such a partition Gandhi would spend his full energies and the rest of his life.

As soon as he was well, he initiated a series of talks with Mohammed Ali Jinnah, president of the Moslem League. The son of a rich merchant, Jinnah had once been a mem-

Riots all over India followed the Mahatma's arrest. Here, police flatten a crowd with smoke bombs.

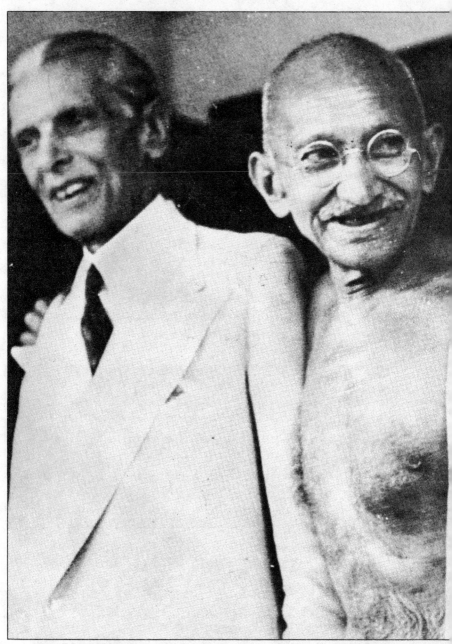

Gandhi and Mohammed Ali Jinnah, leader of 100 million Moslems, at the conclusion of one of their many discussions about the Hindu-Moslem problem. Jinnah had consistently opposed Gandhi since 1920. In 1947, his uncompromising demand that India be partitioned into separate states precipitated a bloody civil war, as Gandhi had known it would.

ber of the All-India Congress and during the twenties had worked with Gandhi for Hindu-Moslem unity. But temperamentally and intellectually he and the Mahatma were at opposite poles. For Jinnah, self-government meant government by an elite of his own kind. His pride could not stand Gandhi's "bottom-up" approach and he had quit the Congress as soon as Gandhi ascended to its leadership.

In 1935, in opposition to a Hindu-dominated Congress, he had formed a coalition with wealthy Moslem landlords and middle-class merchants. Moslems were outnumbered three to one by Hindus, and the fear of all upper-class Moslems was that in an independent India they would lose the patronage they had enjoyed under the British. There was the real possibility, too, that government-enforced programs of land reform would break up their vast estates.

To protect their economic interest, Jinnah proposed that India's one hundred million Moslems be concentrated in an area of vaguely defined boundaries to be known as Pakistan. They hoped to win this territory as a condition of civil peace whenever the British quit India. But their case was only as strong as the evidence of Moslem-Hindu disunity and to build the case Jinnah's League set forth on a deliberate campaign to foment hatred.

In conversations with Jinnah that stretched over seventeen days, the Mahatma tried to negotiate solutions to Moslem-Hindu differences. He pleaded with Jinnah to consider a constitutional form that, while permitting majority rule, would guarantee minority rights. Jinnah—jealous, austere, humorless—steadfastly said no. At one point, Gandhi pled, "You can cut me in two if you wish, but don't cut India in two." Jinnah's answer implied that he would be happy to do both.

In July, 1945, with a Labor Party victory, Clement Attlee replaced Winston Churchill as Prime Minister. Less than a month later, Japan surrendered, and World War II was over. Thereupon Attlee announced steps toward "an early realization of self-government for India." Some months later, a British Cabinet mission arrived for consultations with

Congress and Moslem leaders on plans for independence. When the two factions deadlocked, the mission proceeded to draft its own plan. Its most significant recommendation was that Jinnah's proposal for a separate Moslem state be rejected. It was, in their judgment, "quite impractical."

For four months, the mission labored to make its plan acceptable to both Jinnah and Gandhi.

But Jinnah was too stubborn and Congress leaders were too suspicious, and finally the plan, which would have called for a united India under a single federal constitution, was abandoned. In August, Jinnah, in a fit of petulance, refused to participate further, at which point the viceroy asked Nehru to form a provisional government. This so outraged Jinnah that he proclaimed August 16 as "Moslem Direct Action Day." At an inflammatory press conference, he told Congress, "If you want war, we accept your offer unhesitatingly."

His words came close to sparking a civil war. In Calcutta, aroused Moslems went from a mass meeting into the streets, looting Hindu shops, boasting at the top of their voices that one beef-eating Moslem could lick ten cow-worshiping Hindus, and generally creating disorder. In four days of rioting, five thousand were injured—as many Moslems as Hindus. Two weeks later, Nehru became the provisional Prime Minister. Jinnah proclaimed it a day of mourning and ordered Moslems throughout the country to display black flags, thus enraging the Hindus. For weeks thereafter, violence swept through the provinces. In Noakhali, where Hindus were outnumbered four to one, Moslems murdered hundreds, forcibly converted thousands to Islam, and set fire to more than ten thousand homes. Seeking vengeance, hysterical Hindus in adjacent Bihar set out to kill a hundred outnumbered Moslems for every Hindu killed in Noakhali.

Heartsick, Gandhi felt compelled to act. For most of the past year, he had made his headquarters in a slum dwelling in the untouchables' quarter in Delhi. From there he had participated in the Congress' negotiations with Jinnah and

India's two great leaders enjoy a private chuckle at the opening of the All-India Congress in Bombay, July, 1946.

the British, and had served as a regular adviser to Nehru, whom years before he had named his successor. But he now became convinced that his dream of a united India would never be achieved at the conference table. India could be unified only in the hearts of its people. Most particularly, he believed the time had come for him to appeal directly to the millions of Moslems whom Jinnah claimed as his followers. Somehow, he must also find a way of reminding his own followers of their *Satyagraha* pledge. He would do both, he decided, by an act of unconditional love. He resolved to go to Noakhali. "I won't be at peace with myself until I do," he said.

As if symbolic of the disparate paths to freedom, Nehru and Jinnah took off for London for a conference with Prime Minister Attlee the same month that Gandhi left on a pilgrimage to the most remote villages of East Bengal. Here in one of the most inaccessible regions of India, populated by two million five hundred thousand people, eighty per cent of them Moslems, Gandhi chose to conduct one of the most remarkable ministries of all time. "'Do or die' has to be put to the test here," he wrote. " 'Do' here means Hindus and Moslems should learn to live together in peace and amity. Otherwise, I should die in the attempt." He had just passed his seventy-seventh birthday.

For four months, he walked barefoot from village to village, stopping sometimes as long as two or three days,

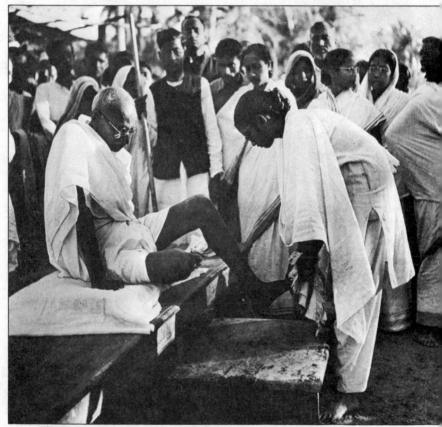

Walking barefoot on a pilgrimage through Noakhali, Gandhi was accompanied by an 18-year-old grand-niece, Manubehn Gandhi, shown here washing his feet. Their relationship was so caring that he regularly introduced her as his grand-daughter.

talking and praying with the natives. He spent his nights as the guest of the first peasant who offered to take him in. He lived on local fruits and vegetables and, when it was available, goat's milk. During the first month he was met by sullen, hostile Moslems who, encouraged by politicians, would precede him on the path, strewing glass, brambles, and dung. He found the Hindus either cowering or fleeing from fear. Wherever he went, he was told of more looting, more murders. Despairing, late in December he wrote a correspondent: "Truth and nonviolence have sustained me for the last sixty years, but today I seem to miss the certainty of that power."

But gradually the people became aware that there was a saint in their midst. Moslem mothers began to bring their sick children to him. A deputation of Moslems who had participated in the recent riots not only asked him for forgiveness but offered to pay their Hindu neighbors for damages. In one village he was acclaimed "the greatest man" and asked to hold his prayer meetings in a Moslem home. A Moslem leader took him to a local mosque. Despite threats from the landlords and politicians, Moslem peasants began to attend his daily prayer meetings in droves. One service was attended by a mixed audience of five thousand.

In all, he lived in forty-nine villages during his four months in Noakhali. Usually he left behind one member of his retinue, sometimes two, to found a hospital or school. Finally, the Hindus who had fled began to return to their homes. It was the clearest sign that, in Noakhali, pacification Gandhi style was working.

But there was only one Gandhi and Noakhali was only a small part of India.

In London, the Prime Minister's conference closed with a warning from Jinnah that if the issue was not settled soon on terms that would provide for an independent Pakistan, Moslems and Hindus would "wash the continent" with one another's blood. Alarmed, Prime Minister Attlee told the House of Commons that England would quit India "not

With Lord and Lady Mountbatten outside the Viceroy's House, New Delhi, in March, 1947.

later than June, 1948." To speed the departure, he dispatched the famous war hero, Lord Louis Mountbatten, to Delhi, as the twentieth and last British viceroy.

Gandhi returned from Noakhali in March to begin a round of five fateful conferences with Mountbatten. Very quickly, the issue crystallized: According to Jinnah, civil war would be inevitable if the British did not leave India divided into Hindu and Moslem states; according to Gandhi, civil war would be inevitable if Britain failed to guarantee a free and unified India.

By June, Gandhi was alone and isolated. Wearying of the struggle, anxious to put an end to the continuing violence, impatient for the self-rule that now after so many years seemed at hand, Nehru and the other elected officials agreed to a compromise plan of partition. In effect, Moslem Pakistan was to be created by bisecting the great provinces of Bengal and the Punjab. On June 3, Mountbatten announced the details of a plan that also had the approval of the Moslem League.

It did not, however, have Gandhi's approval. "Nobody can force me to accept it except God," he said sadly. He felt that thirty-two years of work had come "to an inglorious end."

August 15, 1947, was Independence Day for India. But Gandhi refused an invitation to the inaugural ceremonies in Delhi. He stayed in Calcutta, where he had been trying to calm the rioters, and he spent the day fasting and in prayer. He had not given up. "No cause that is intrinsically just can ever be described as forlorn," he decided. "I am a born fighter who does not know failure." His India need not be permanently divided. He would find a way to reclaim Pakistan. His dream could be redeemed.

But with the reality of partition came the full-scale civil war that he had feared and predicted. No matter how the lines were drawn, some Moslems remained in Hindu territory and some Hindus were trapped in Pakistan. In the Punjab the partition line ran through the heart of a prosperous community of five million Sikhs, a sect of reformed Hindus with an earned reputation for ferocity in warfare. Fierce battles ensued when Moslems on the Pakistan side tried to drive the Sikhs from their land. As if by reflex the Sikhs on the Indian side turned on the millions of Moslems remaining in east Punjab, killing them or driving them into Pakistan. Out of one caravan of one hundred thousand Moslem refugees, only four thousand reached Pakistan alive.

The Mahatma's presence in Calcutta had a calming effect on troubled Bengal. There, millions of Moslems were able to celebrate a holy festival in safety, without harrassment from their Hindu enemies. But the calm was deceptively short-lived. By the end of August, tempers had once again been dangerously aroused. The seething masses, enraged by fresh reports of atrocities on both sides, could hear nothing but cries for vengeance. Hindu fanatics were particularly infuriated by Gandhi's appeals to "forgive and forget" and became more and more open with the charge that he was an unconscious agent of the Moslems. One night a howling mob of Hindus broke into the house where he was staying, in such a frenzy it took police with tear gas to disperse them. Gandhi narrowly escaped injury in his futile effort to quiet them.

Reflecting unhappily on his inability to make himself

Visiting a New Delhi camp, Gandhi was cheered by 50,000 Moslem refugees awaiting transportation to Pakistan.

heard above the yelling crowd, Gandhi decided to speak to India in the most personal way he knew—by fasting. After a light meal on the evening of September 1, he announced that he would not eat again until "sanity returns to Calcutta." Seventy-three hours later he broke his fast when in his presence Hindu, Moslem, and Christian delegations signed collective vows to keep the peace. It is a matter of record that from that day on, during the months when most other provinces were turbulent with fratricide, there were no more riots in Bengal.

Elsewhere in India began what came to be called the Great Migration, in which no less than fifteen million displaced Indians walked, crept, or rode across hundreds of miles in panicky search for friendly territory. Out of Pakistan came millions of Hindus and Sikhs fleeing in the general direction of Delhi. From the new India moved a long convoy of homeless Moslems, bound for Pakistan. Both Moslems and Hindus were alternately the oppressed and the oppressor. Before hostilities ran their course, at least 600,000 people were massacred. "Both sides have gone crazy," said Gandhi in anguish.

In a situation generally demoralized, the most sinister factor was the rise of a terrorist, totalitarian Hindu organization of young men called the RSS (the Rashtriya Sevak Sangha). Under the banner of "Akand Hindustan" (Indivisible India), RSS members plotted military conquest of Pakistan and launched a systematic campaign to exterminate all Moslems in the new India. Its appeal was formidable; one of its rallies in Delhi attracted a crowd of fifty thousand.

Four days after his fast, Gandhi left Calcutta for the Punjab, where the terror was at its worst. En route, he was persuaded to stop at Delhi where the influx of thousands of refugees had provoked uncontrollable rioting. Because the slum where he customarily stayed in Delhi was overrun by hooligans, he set up his base in the palatial home of a wealthy industrialist, G. D. Birla. From there, for the next three months, he moved through the streets of Delhi, now the city of the mad and the dead, taking his gospel of love into both hostile camps. His efforts were only partially successful. Although rioting had greatly diminished, any Moslem faced the possibility of being murdered any time he stepped outdoors. On January 13, 1948, in a last effort to halt the violence, Gandhi began a "fast unto death." It was his twentieth fast, his seventh major one, and it was to be his last.

He was seventy-eight and his friends and doctors were convinced that a long fast would kill him. "Rather death," he told them "than that I should be a helpless witness to the destruction of India, Hinduism, Sikhs, and Islam." He would break the fast "when and if I'm satisfied that there is a reunion of hearts of all the communities."

He had another purpose in mind, too. At the time of partitioning, new India had agreed to pay Pakistan about $180 million, a sum equivalent to Pakistan's share of the Indian treasury before independence. Now, under a generally "get tough" policy toward what it viewed as a potential enemy, the Nehru cabinet had decided to cancel its commitment. By fasting, Gandhi hoped to shame the government into doing what it had promised to do.

The fast lasted six days, during which time leaders of the religious communities and political factions met in round-the-clock sessions in an effort to agree on a statement of reconciliation that would satisfy the Mahatma. All over the country there were spontaneous demonstrations of Moslem-Hindu good will, almost enough to drown out the sound of counter-demonstrations from Hindu extremists. On the evening of the first day he was able to conduct his usual prayer meeting on the grounds of Birla House. On the second day, unable to walk the distance, he dictated a message to the congregation. By the third day he was in great pain and too weak to move.

That night the Indian Cabinet reversed its earlier decision and voted to pay Pakistan the $180 million. Three days later, Hindu, Sikh, Christian, Moslem, and Jewish leaders, including the High Commissioner of Pakistan and a leader of the RSS, signed a communal pact, pledging restoration of

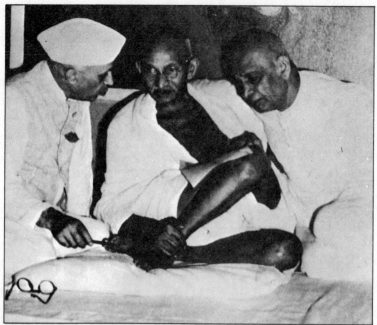

Final meeting with his two old friends, Nehru and Sardar Patel. The assassination is said to have occurred shortly after this meeting.

mosques and Mohammedan businesses and guaranteeing free circulation of Moslems throughout Delhi. Immediately thereafter, a delegation of more than a hundred motored to Birla House.

As they grouped themselves around his cot, the Mahatma rose feebly to his familiar cross-legged sitting position. He was silent and almost expressionless as the Congress president read and explained the pledge. When they asked him if he would now break his fast, he searched their faces and shook his head. It would be a mistake, he said, for him to give up the fast "if you hold yourselves responsible for the communal peace in Delhi only." Overcome by weakness, he began to weep.

Recovering but unable to find his voice, he whispered his questions to his doctor, who repeated them aloud to the crowd. Were they sincere, or were they merely trying to save his life? Did Moslems still regard Hindus as idol-worshiping infidels? Would the RSS abandon its program to exterminate the Moslems? Would they combine their influence to keep the peace throughout all of India and Pakistan? One after the other, the leading Moslem in the Congress, the RSS spokesman, the High Commissioner of Pakistan, and a tall, blue-turbaned Sikh stepped forward, pleading, each offering his own words of assurance.

Gandhi listened thoughtfully. When they were finished, he continued to sit in silence for a long while. Every occupant in the room stood tense and anxious, fearful that the Mahatma might have chosen to die. Finally, he gave a funny little smile and nodded. Instantly, the room was noisy with the laughing, tearful sounds of relief. A moment later, *ashramites* led the group in one of Gandhi's typical religious services, reading from the scriptures of all religions

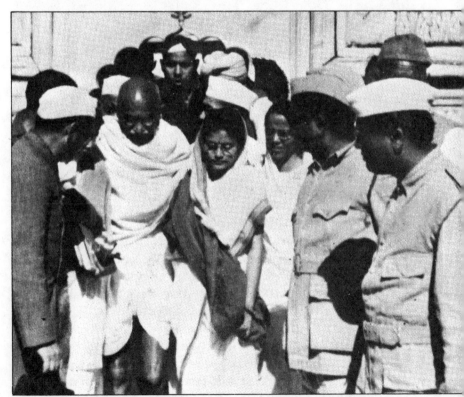

At the Mohammedan Shrine in New Delhi. This photograph is believed to be the last one taken of him before his death.

and closing with one of his favorite hymns, "When I Survey the Wondrous Cross." Ceremoniously, a Moslem handed the Mahatma a glass of orange juice. The fast was over.

On January 20, the outdoor prayer meeting was disturbed by an explosion from a homemade bomb tossed from a near-by garden wall. The police arrested a Punjab refugee who said he had been enlisted by the RSS to kill the Mahatma.

Unruffled, Gandhi continued to hold prayer meetings in the garden. To those who congratulated him for his composure, he said: "I would deserve praise only if I fell as a result of such an explosion and yet retained a smile on my face and no malice for the doer." He forgave the bomb-thrower and asked the police not to "molest" him. He would allow the government neither to provide him with a guard nor to search the worshipers.

The following Sunday his prayer meeting was unusually well attended. He read from the Koran and asked each Hindu and Sikh in the audience to bring along "at least one Moslem" to prayers thereafter. He announced that his next journey on behalf of peace would be to Pakistan.

Did he have a premonition of death? On January 29, he told a member of the *ashram:* "If I die of a lingering ill-ness . . . it will be your duty to proclaim to the world, even at the risk of making people angry with you, that I was not the man of God that I claimed to be . . . Note down this also—that if someone were to end my life by putting a bullet through me . . . and I met his bullet without a groan and breathed my last taking God's name—then alone would I have made good my claim."

The next day, at four in the afternoon, he was visited by Sardar Patel, strong man of the Congress Party. They continued to talk through his four-thirty supper of goat's milk. oranges, and raw vegetables. At five, with an expression of self-reproach, he rose and asked his two grand-nieces to escort him to prayer. "I am late by ten minutes," he said peevishly. "I hate being late."

Quickly, he made his way across the open grass and

The funeral procession heads toward Rajghat on the banks of the Jamuna River where the cremation was to take place. Afterward, the Mahatma's ashes were immersed in the holy river Ganges.

mounted the five steps that led to the prayer ground. Five hundred people were waiting. Among them was a thirty-five-year-old member of the RSS, the editor and publisher of a radical weekly newspaper in Poona. His name was Nathuram Vinayak Godse. He had a pistol in his pocket.

Upon Gandhi's appearance, the congregation drew back, just enough to make him a pathway. Some pressed closer, touching him as he passed; many bowed at his feet. Smiling, he murmured his apologies for being late and touched his palms together in the traditional Hindu gesture. At that moment Godse stepped forward. Before pulling out his revolver, he bowed low as if in reverence. He then fired three times into Gandhi's stomach and heart. Gandhi fell, murmuring the words *"He Rama"*—"O God" and making the sign of forgiveness. He died immediately. By his own stringent terms, expressed to a disciple twenty hours before, he had made good his claim.

Afterword

They "honored" him with a military funeral.

From Birla House his anointed body was transported for cremation to a spot on the bank of the Jamuna River nine miles away. For a bier they gave him a flower-bedecked weapons carrier. For an escort, they gave him splendidly uniformed men of the Indian army, navy, and air force. Tanks and armored cars led the procession. Behind them came Lord Mountbatten's bemedaled bodyguard, a mounted cavalry unit, and a company of riflemen. Overhead, Dakotas of the Royal Indian Air Force dipped in salute and let loose showers of scented blossoms.

However ironic the ceremony may have been for the last rites of a man who had spent his life preaching peace and simplicity, it served eloquently to dramatize the pragmatism of Gandhi's onetime deputies who were now the leaders of free India. *Nonviolence is fine for winning independence*, went their message to the world; *it is unthinkable as a policy of state.*

THERE ARE THOSE who maintain that Gandhi was a phenomenon peculiar to his time and place. He could have done what he did only in India, they insist; only against a conscience-stricken power like Britain and only during an era of faltering colonialism. Nonviolence, they say, may be a laudable concept but it is as contrary to human nature as it is to the nature of governments.

There are others, however, who argue that Gandhi was really ahead of his time, that his ideas have more relevance for the future than they did even in his lifetime. There are clergymen who see in his approach to religion the inspiration for the current ecumenical movement of religious reconciliation. There are political theorists who since his death have come to see *Satyagraha*—or some form of ritualized nonviolence—as the only realistic alternative to nuclear warfare and global annihilation. There are urban planners in America who find in his village experiments promising models for population dispersal and government decentralization.

But Gandhi's most important contribution may ultimately turn out to be not to religion, politics, or sociology, but to psychology—to our understanding of ourselves and particularly of our potential for personal growth. For what Gandhi did, most of all, was to give us a new vision of man. "Nonviolence is the law of our species," he maintained, and he lived his life to prove that it could be. Most especially, he demonstrated man's capacity to change. In a technological age where change is likely to be equated with survival, the lesson could be crucial.

The personal possessions that Mahatma Gandhi left behind.

Books for Further Reading

ASHE, GEOFFREY, *Gandhi*. New York: Stein and Day, 1968.

FISCHER, LOUIS, *Gandhi, His Life and Message for the World*. New York: The New American Library, 1954.

———, *The Essential Gandhi*. New York: Random House, 1962.

GANDHI, MOHANDAS K., *The Story of My Experiments with Truth, an Autobiography*. Boston: Beacon Press, 1957.

———, *All Men Are Brothers*. Paris: United Nations Educational, Scientific, and Cultural Organization, 1958.

GREGG, RICHARD B., *The Power of Nonviolence*. Philadelphia: J. B. Lippincott Company, 1935.

HUTHEESING, KRISHNA NEHRU, with ALDEN HATCH, *We Nehrus*. New York: Holt, Rinehart and Winston, 1967.

MOSLEY, LEONARD, *The Last Days of the British Raj*. New York: Harcourt, Brace & World, 1961.

MASCARO, JUAN, Introduction by. *Bhagavad-Gita*. Baltimore: Penguin Books, 1962.

NANDA, B. R., *Mahatma Gandhi*. London: George Allen & Unwin, Ltd., 1965. (Distributed in U. S. through Barron's Educational Series, Inc., Woodbury, New York.)

NEHRU, JAWAHARLAL, *Nehru on Gandhi*. New York: The John Day Company, 1948.

PRABHAVANANDA, SWAMI, and CHRISTOPHER ISHERWOOD, Translated by. *Bhagavad-Gita, The Song of God.* Introduction by Aldous Huxley. New York: The New American Library, 1954.

WALLBANK, T. WALTER, *A Short History of India and Pakistan.* New York: The New American Library, 1965.

WOFFORD, CLARE and HARRIS, *India Afire.* New York: The John Day Company, 1961.

Since publication of the first edition of *Gandhi, Soldier of Nonviolence,* three other works have appeared, each a significant contribution to the understanding of Gandhi's teachings and continuing influence on Western thought:

ERICKSON, ERIK H., *Gandhi's Truth.* New York: W.W. Norton & Co., 1969.

MEHTA, VED, *Mahatma Gandhi and His Apostles.* New York: Penguin Books, Inc., 1977.

PAYNE, ROBERT, *The Life and Death of Mahatma Gandhi.* New York: E.P. Dutton & Co., 1969.

Index

Index

A Note About the Author

CALVIN KYTLE'S interest in Gandhi was stimulated by his experiences in 1964–65 when, as acting director of a federal conciliation agency, the U.S. Community Relations Service, he saw first-hand the enormous impact of the Mahatma's teachings on the civil-rights movement in the South. Before coming to Washington, he was an executive with the Nationwide Insurance Companies of Columbus, Ohio, for a while serving as the officer in charge of both personnel and public relations. Before that he was a newspaperman in Georgia. He now heads his own communications firm, working mostly with nonprofit groups in the design and publicizing of research studies centered on problems of urban affairs, the environment, energy, and public education. A native of South Carolina, he is a graduate of Atlanta's Emory University, where he also taught journalism briefly. Over the years he has been an occasional contributor to many national magazines, including *Harper's* and *Saturday Review*.

Martin Luther King at Gandhi's shrine. Rajghat, 1959.

CHRISTIAN HERALD ASSOCIATION AND ITS MINISTRIES

CHRISTIAN HERALD ASSOCIATION, founded in 1878, publishes The Christian Herald Magazine, one of the leading interdenominational religious monthlies in America. Through its wide circulation, it brings inspiring articles and the latest news of religious developments to many families. From the magazine's pages came the initiative for CHRISTIAN HERALD CHILDREN'S HOME and THE BOWERY MISSION, two individually supported not-for-profit corporations.

CHRISTIAN HERALD CHILDREN'S HOME, established in 1894, is the name for a unique and dynamic ministry to disadvantaged children, offering hope and opportunities which would not otherwise be available for reasons of poverty and neglect. The goal is to develop each child's potential and to demonstrate Christian compassion and understanding to children in need.

Mont Lawn is a permanent camp located in Bushkill, Pennsylvania. It is the focal point of a ministry which provides a healthful "vacation with a purpose" to children who without it would be confined to the streets of the city. Up to 1000 children between the ages of 7 and 11 come to Mont Lawn each year.

Christian Herald Children's Home maintains year-round contact with children by means of an *In-City Youth Ministry*. Central to its philosophy is the belief that only through sustained relationships and demonstrated concern can individual lives be truly enriched. Special emphasis is on individual guidance, spiritual and family counseling and tutoring. This follow-up ministry to inner-city children culminates for many in financial assistance toward higher education and career counseling.

THE BOWERY MISSION, located at 227 Bowery, New York City, has since 1879 been reaching out to the lost men on the Bowery, offering them what could be their last chance to rebuild their lives. Every man is fed, clothed and ministered to. Countless numbers have entered the 90-day residential rehabilitation program at the Bowery Mission. A concentrated ministry of counseling, medical care, nutrition therapy, Bible study and Gospel services awakens a man to spiritual renewal within himself.

These ministries are supported solely by the voluntary contributions of individuals and by legacies and bequests. Contributions are tax deductible. Checks should be made out either to CHRISTIAN HERALD CHILDREN'S HOME or to THE BOWERY MISSION.

Administrative Office: 40 Overlook Drive, Chappaqua, New York 10514
Telephone: (914) 769-9000